# seven wonders of grace

## C.H. SPURGEON

D1158529

**BAKER BOOK HOUSE**
Grand Rapids, Michigan

Paperback edition issued 1978
by Baker Book House
from the edition issued
by Passmore and Alabaster

ISBN: 0-8010-8131-9

PHOTOLITHOPRINTED BY CUSHING - MALLOY, INC.
ANN ARBOR, MICHIGAN, UNITED STATES OF AMERICA
1978

# PREFACE

---

HE who never wonders has no mind. "The wise man only wonders once in his life, and that is always." This is specially true of the kingdom of grace, where everything is marvellous. When the great God comes to deal with offending men in the way of mercy the mere idea of such grace is wonderful, but when he for the sake of sinners gives his Son to die it is a world of wonders in one.

A dogmatic writer has said that "all wonder is but the effect of novelty upon ignorance," but assuredly it is not so when the work of redemption is the theme ; here the more we know the more we wonder, and years of familiar acquaintance and growing understanding do but increase our astonishment. The name whereby our ever-blessed Lord is called is "Wonderful," and well does he deserve the title, for his person, his birth, his life, his death, his teachings, and his actions are all wonderful. Out of the proclamation of the amazing story of the love of Jesus other wonders grow, for signs and wonders are the witnesses of the gospel's power. Newborn souls are "set for wonders in Israel"; and those who delight to search out the glorious works of the Lord are filled with holy admiration and astonishment as they see the heart and hand of the Lord revealed in each individual.

To set forth some of the "wonders of grace" this little book was prepared. Come, reader, and see the various characters upon which grace operates, and it may be, if you are unsaved, you will find here a something to arouse or to encourage you. May the Holy Spirit bless these our utterances to the souls of many, and lead them to the wonder-working Lord who of his own free grace forgives sin, renews the heart, and preserves the spirit. We have said in our heart, "Surely I will remember thy wonders of old," and here is the result of our musings.

Reader, if thou be a regenerated man or woman, pray for

Thy servant in Christ,

C. H. SPURGEON

# CONTENTS

# MANASSEH;

## OR,

## THE OUTRAGEOUS REBEL

"And when he was in affliction, he besought the Lord his God, and humbled himself greatly before the God of his fathers, and prayed unto him: and he was intreated of him, and heard his supplication, and brought him again to Jerusalem into his kingdom. Then Manasseh knew that the Lord he was God."—2 Chronicles xxxiii. 12, 13.

WHEN we wish to recommend a physician to a friend who is very ill we are in the habit of mentioning certain cures which he has wrought; and when we can produce several astonishing instances we feel that we are going the right way to work to convince the judgment of our friend and to win his confidence in the doctor. Now, it is our impression that very many are anxious to be saved by the grace of

God who, nevertheless, have not dared to
trust the great Healer of souls : they know
that they are in great danger, but they
are reluctant to go to " the beloved physician." They are grievously afraid because
of the greatness of their sins, and they
are filled with doubt and unbelief as to
the possibility of their salvation on account
of their singular sinfulness. Therefore
it struck me that if I could set before
them a number of Scriptural instances of
wonderful conversions it might tend to
encourage hope in Christ in their hearts,
and, under the blessing of the Holy Spirit,
it might be the means of leading them to
trust and try our Lord Jesus, out of whose
very garment virtue flows. Perhaps, dear
friends, as you shall see how the Lord, the
Healer, has looked on one and another, and
restored them from the horrible disease of
sin, you, too, who feel yourselves far gone,
may pluck up courage and say, " If he
healed others, why should he not also heal
me ? I too will touch his garment's hem
and see if he will not make me perfectly
whole." How I wish that poor souls
knew how ready my Lord Jesus is to save
them : they would not keep back if they
knew how eager he is to have mercy on

the guilty. I pine within my soul to lead you to Jesus that you may be blest. That is the desire of my heart in introducing to you the case of Manasseh, whom I select from the Old Testament as a very prominent instance of glaring sin and of amazing grace.

We do not find many of what we can accurately call conversions in the Old Testament. It is a record of a dim dispensation in which we rather see the types of things than the things themselves; but I should suppose that the priests, if they had been inspired to write what they often heard, would have been able to tell of many instances of deep conviction which would be made known in connection with the sin offerings and the trespass offerings, and they probably saw many instances of persons who henceforth led a new life and ceased from the sin which they had confessed over the victim's head. Of conviction, confession, and conversion they must have seen a great deal, but records we have none. On this account the story of the madly wicked king who was led to humble himself greatly before God is all the more valuable, and it is matter for thankfulness that it is so remarkable.

Every item of it reflects glory upon the amazing grace of God, and, indeed, compels us to exclaim, " Who is a God like unto thee, passing by transgression, iniquity, and sin ? "

We will waste no time on a preface, but come at once to the life-story of Manasseh, and look, first, at *his circumstances;* then consider him as *a great sinner;* and afterwards, with greater comfort, view him as *a remarkable convert.*

I. First, let us notice HIS CIRCUMSTANCES ; because a man's sin may be heightened by his position, or on the other hand, the condition in which he is placed may suggest some alleviating considerations which, in all fairness, should be remembered. Now, with regard to Manasseh, we find that *he was the child of an eminently godly father:* the son of a king who, with all his mistakes, was sound in heart towards God. Hezekiah "wrought that which was good, and right, and truth before the Lord his God." He was a man mighty in prayer, and found deliverance thereby in the hour of great peril through the invasion of Sennacherib, a man whose life was so precious in the sight of the Lord that, in answer to his cries, he gave

him a new lease of life, and spared him
yet another fifteen years. It is a great
thing for a youth to have a godly father
to train his tender mind; and, even
though such a parent should be early taken
away, yet the privilege is an eminent
one. As for Manasseh's mother, we cannot
say with certainty that she was a godly
woman, but let us hope that as her name
was Hephzibah—"My delight is in her"
—she, too, was delightful for grace and
piety. Isaiah seems to have taken her
name and to have applied it to the church:
"thou shalt be called Hephzibah, for the
Lord delighteth in thee," and we may
suppose that he would hardly have done
so unless there had been some sweet associations therewith. Let us trust that
Queen Hephzibah was indeed God's delight; and, if so, Manasseh had the special
favour of having two parents who would
train him up in the way he should go.
Such a happy start in life renders his
after sin the more heinous.

But, in all truthfulness, we have to
mention next that *he was a child born to
his father in his later years*, after his life
had been lengthened by special license
from above. He was the child of his

parent's desire, an heir born after the
father had expected to die childless, and
therefore, it is not at all unlikely that he
was a spoiled child. It is very possible
that being highly prized he was also
greatly indulged, and if so he was in
special danger. Those children who are
doted upon by their parents are greatly to
be pitied, for they are apt to be allowed to
have their own way, and a youth's own
way is sure to be a wrong one. Fathers,
in such cases, are apt to play the part of
Eli, of whom we read that his sons made
themselves vile, and he restrained them
not. It was no wonder that Adonijah
disturbed the dying moments of David
when we read that " his father had not
displeased him at any time in saying, Why
hast thou done so ?" Nor need we marvel
that Absalom almost broke his father's
heart, if this was the manner of his bringing up. Even though at twelve years of
age Manasseh could not have fully developed his character, yet it may have been
warped by those early days of admiration
and indulgence. Parents, take note of
this, and you petted children do the same.
Recollect that *Manasseh lost his father
at twelve years of age.* I do not know a

greater trial for a family than for the head of the house to be taken away while the children are young. Just when the guiding, encouraging, and restraining power of the father is wanted it is mournful to see it removed. How mysterious it seems to us when a large family loses the wise guide of the household at the very time when his influence is most needed by the up-growing boys and girls. Too often in such a case the young people have broken away from all restraint, and the loss of their father has been the loss of everything. Manasseh, the prince who seemed born under such favourable circumstances for the production of a gracious character, was much to be pitied when the good king his father was called away, and his tender son was left alone amid flatterers and idolaters.

Remember, too, that *Manasseh was placed in a giddy position as a child*, for he mounted the throne at twelve years of age. A child upon a throne is a child out of its natural place. Such high and hard places are not for boys. Now and then such a child turns out to be a Josiah, the very delight of mankind ; but the pro-babilities are very much against its being so. " Woe unto thee, O land, when thy king is a child," It is ill for a child to sway a sceptre, but " it is good for a man that he bear the yoke in his youth." A fierce fire of temptation blazes around a youthful throne. Sycophants and flatterers are sure to surround a boy prince, pandering to his worst desires, and arousing that part of his nature which most needs to be repressed. No doubt there were good people whom Hezekiah had gathered in his courts, but then they could not flatter so well as the evil party which had been repressed for awhile but still remained strong in the land. Though Hezekiah had set up the worship of God everywhere, and had done his best to root out idolatry, yet the idolatrous party was far from being extinct, and the common people were sadly careless and irreligious. Isaiah in his opening chapter describes the condition of the land by saying, " Israel doth not know, my people doth not consider." " Except the Lord of hosts had left unto us a very small remnant, we should have been as Sodom, and we should have been like unto Gomorrah." The nation was not steadfast like king Hezekiah : it worshipped Jehovah when compelled by royal authority, but it was ready enough to turn aside to its idols. The idolatrous party— which I might liken to the papists; and the people who worshipped on the high places—who were the ritualistic party of the day; came around the young king, fawning, flattering, and cajoling. By pleasing the taste of the boy-king, and indulging his vices, they undermined in his esteem the orthodox worshippers of God, whom I may call the evangelical school. He yielded himself up readily to their influence, and when he was old enough became the head of the idolatrous party, throwing his whole soul into it, and, with all the might of his nature, and the force of his authority labouring to stamp out the pure worship of the most high God, and to set up those debasing idolatries which his father Hezekiah had so much abhorred. Look at him, then, as a mere child placed in a condition of great danger, led astray at first, and afterwards becoming a ring-leader in iniquity.

If I should address any young person who finds himself, too early for his good, set free from the restraint of parents and placed in a position of considerable power and influence over others, I pray him to flee to the Lord for help, or his ruin will be certain. The Lord can teach the young men wisdom, the babes knowledge and discretion. Look to your Bible, the mercy-seat, and your God, or you will make shipwreck of the life which God has entrusted to you. There are responsibilities upon you too heavy for you to carry alone : because your burdens are heavier seek for yourself more power from on high : because your restraints are fewer put yourself under the restraints of divine love. The youth who is so much trusted by providence as to be left alone without a guardian, and to have power confided to him which usually needs the wisdom of age, ought to be the more careful and the more guarded, and cry the more earnestly to God that he may have grace given to him, lest of him it should be said, as it was said of Manasseh, he " did evil in the sight of the Lord."

These are some of the circumstances of Manasseh's life.

II. Now I have a heavy task, and one which saddens me, though it is concerning one who lived so many hundreds of years ago : I have mournfully to describe Manasseh as A GREAT SINNER. If you will turn to the Second of Chronicles, chapter xxxiii. and will follow the verses, you will get a view of this atrocious offender. In the second verse we read, " *He did that which was evil in the sight of the Lord.*" That is a description of his life as a whole. Take his fifty-five years' reign in the bulk, notwithstanding the repentance of his later years, it is a true estimate of it all to say that " he did evil in the sight of the Lord." He was a son of David, but he was the very reverse of that king, who was always faithful in his loyalty to the one only God of Israel. David's blood was in his veins, but David's ways were not in his heart. He was a wild, degenerate shoot of a noble vine.

Nay, the description of his life is more intensely black than the summary might suggest, for it is said that " he did evil in the sight of the Lord, like unto the abominations of the heathen, whom the Lord had cast out before the children of Israel." He seemed to have taken for his models the men whom God condemned to die for capital offences against his law. How deplorable that one who was cradled in piety must, notwithstanding, not be satisfied until the

very scum of society, which God had
skimmed off as from the pot and thrown
away with detestation, should be his
models and his tutors. Yet we have
known young men to be doubly perverse,
possessed as it were by the devil, if not
by seven devils at once. We are all depraved, but in some that depravity mani-
fests itself in an extraordinary love of low,
coarse society, and of everything that is
irreligious and unlovely. I have in my
mind's eye now—and it makes my heart
melt as I remember it—sons of men with
whom I have been glad to associate, and
who were always happy to aid me in the
Lord's work, but now their sons find
their most congenial company amongst the
drunken and profane, the gamblers and de-
bauchees ; and if perchance they see their
father's friend they look aside or slink
away, anxious to be unobserved by him,
scarcely brooking to have it known that
they know the man. This is the unhap-
piest thing that can occur to us parents.
You who have buried your little children,
you who have wept so bitterly when your
dear babes were snatched from your
bosoms, may far prefer that sorrow to
having your sons and your daughters live

to dishonour your name by plunging into glaring sin. Manasseh was a son of this character, and could his father have foreseen what he would live to do he would have preferred death rather than have lived to be the sire of such a monster of iniquity.

It is noted concerning him, in the next place, that *he undid what his father had done.* In the third verse we read, " He built again the high places which Hezekiah, his father, had broken down." I have known many a man who has had no respect for God who, nevertheless, has had such a regard for his father's memory that he would not scoff at things which his father held sacred. But this man had cast off all filial reverence. He cared not what his godly parent might have thought, he gloried in building up what his father had thrown down, and throwing down what his father had built up.

This is a great evil ; for a man in order to be guilty of it has to do violence to some of the strongest and best instincts of his nature. Is that your case, my friend ? Are you doing exactly that which you know would have broken your father's heart ? Is your conduct such that your

mother would have been brought to her
grave by it had she been here? Are you
fighting against the Lord God of your
father? May the Lord in mercy stay
your guilty hand lest the curse of Absalom come upon you. Turn not aside from
your father's God, follow in the godly
footsteps of your mother, and set not
yourself to act contemptuously against
that which was your parents' reverence.

*Manasseh next sinned in a great variety
of ways,* for, according to the third verse,
he seemed eager to be meddling with all
forms of idolatry. He was not satisfied
with one false god, or one set of idolatrous
rites, but he reared up altars for Baalim
and made groves, and worshipped the host
of heaven ; nor yet content with all this
he adored Moloch, and passed his children
through the fire in the valley of the son of
Hinnom. He heaped up vile idolatries,
not only sending far and wide to find out
what were the gods of the different nations, but reviving the old cast-off gods
of the Canaanites, whom God had destroyed for their crimes. One form of
insult to the living God was not enough
for him, he heaped together his rebellions.
There are men to whom to sin with one

hand is not sufficient : they must trans-
gress with greediness. One vice does not
content them, they cannot be satisfied to
go to hell except with four steeds to their
chariot, and these they drive like Jehu
the furious. They never seem content
except with all their might they are fighting against the Lord, and pulling down
his wrath upon their heads.

These sins of Manasseh were not merely
various, but *some of them were peculiarly
foul.* The worship of Baalim and Ashtaroth was associated with such abominations that one is sorry even to have known
of them, and especially the *ashera,* or
symbols, wrongly translated " groves,"
were so lascivious that I shall not so
much as hint at what they were. Such
worship must have unutterably defiled
the mind of the worshipper, and rendered
him fit for vice of the most degrading
kind. Think of obscenity made into a
religion : vice an ingredient of adoration.
O God ! that ever man should have come
down to this ! Worse still that a king of
Judah and a son of Hezekiah should
patronize and ordain orgies which polluted
the mind beyond conception. It sufficed
not that he adored the sun when it shined,

and kissed his hand to the moon walking
in her brightness; the sin of star worship
was not enough, but he must needs set up
graven images and worship the idols of
the Philistines, of Egypt, Assyria, and
Tyre. The calves of Bethel did not sufficiently provoke the Lord, but the idols of
Baal and the lewdness of Ashtaroth must
defile the whole land from end to end.
Instead of the holy worship of Jehovah
the worship of devils was ordained by the
king's authority, and Judah's land became
a den of abominations.

But Manasseh went to the utmost in
evil, and *added gross impudence and insult to his crimes*, so as to defy the Lord
to his face, for " he built altars in the
house of the Lord, whereof the Lord had
said, In Jerusalem shall my name be for
ever. And he built altars for all the host of
heaven in the two courts of the house of
the Lord." Oh, the infinite patience of the
Most High, that he bore with such a
daring insult as this! There were all the
hills of Judah and the valleys thereof.
Were they not enough for Manasseh's
idols and their altars? Must the hill of
Zion also be profaned? Was there no
spot but that which the Lord had set

apart for himself, and of which it had been said, "The Lord is there"? Must Jehovah's own courts be desecrated with the image of jealousy? Must the altars to the hosts of heaven be set up where only the Lord of hosts should have been adored! Yet Manasseh dared to do this, carrying rebellion against the Lord to its utmost extent.

Another proof of his inveterate sinfulness is found *in his treatment of his children:* he was not satisfied with sinning in his own person, his offspring must be handed over to the evil one. "He caused his children to pass through the fire in the valley of the son of Hinnom." Moloch is said to have been represented by a great hollow image made of brass, which was heated red hot and filled with fire till the flames came pouring forth from its mouth. Into the red-hot arms of this image some parents placed their babes, so that they were consumed alive; but others, like Manasseh, passed their children between these burning arms, so that they received "a baptism of fire." It was a cruel consecration of the poor helpless infants to the monstrous demon Moloch, whose altar stood conspicuous in the valley of Hinnom,

outside the walls of Jerusalem. It was
an atrocious crime that children, and children of the seed of Abraham, who were
under covenant with God according to the
flesh, should be thus profanely made to
share in abominable rites. Yet nothing
would content this man but that his own
children should be the sworn adversaries of
God, and from their birth be scorched in
unhallowed flames. Alas, Manasseh is not
alone, for many fathers and mothers seem
bent upon ruining their children's souls.
What shall I say of the man who teaches
his boy to drink, who instructs him in vice
by his example, and compels him to learn
profanity from his father's lips? Can
anything be worse? How much better is
the woman who consecrates her daughter
to fashion, and all its follies, and teaches
her worldliness, love of finery, gaiety, and
vain company? Do not many train their
boys to avarice and their girls to be lovers
of pleasure? I might say even worse, but
surely the passing of children through the
fire to Bacchus, to Mammon, to Venus, to
the very devil himself, is common enough
still, and who shall estimate the enormity
of the crime?

Nor is this all. *Manasseh went to ex-*

*tremes in personal, deliberate sin,* for it is said of him that for himself, and on his own account, he "observed times"—that is "lucky" and "unlucky" days, and he "used enchantments"—those different devices by which men think they can produce certain events or foretell them. "And he used witchcraft, and dealt with a familiar spirit, and with wizards." It matters nothing whether these things were deceits by which he was duped, or were real dealings with demons—the sin is the same, because in the man's intent forbidden intercourse was carried on, such intercourse as is abominable in the sight of the Most High, and to be abhorred by every believer. Whether true or pretended, attempts at necromancy, and witchcraft, and communion with spirits mark a mind far gone astray from God. Remember that such persons cannot enter heaven, for "without are dogs and sorcerers," and they are placed with whoremongers and liars, who are declared to be shut out of the holy city. Manasseh was eager and greedy in these detestable pursuits, he could never have enough of them. Witches, wizards, familiar spirits, enchantments, all sorts of cheats he trusted in : he who would not believe in God could freely yield his faith to lying wonders. How sad to see a mind capable of thought and reason bowed down at the feet of witches and mutterers of spells! How horrible to see a man making a league with death and a covenant with hell! Still, if a man should have gone this length he may yet be recovered out of the snare of the devil by almighty grace. Friend, if you have even wandered into this infamous wickedness you need not despair, for Jesus lives to save the vilest of the vile.

The picture is awful enough already, surely, say you. Ay, but we have other strokes to add, for Manasseh *repeated these sins and exaggerated them each time.* After one forbidden idol had been enshrined he set up another yet more foul, and after building altars in the courts of the temple he ventured further, and " set a carved image, the idol which he had made, in the house of God, of which God had said to David and to Solomon his son, In this house, and in Jerusalem, which I have chosen before all the tribes of Israel, will I put my name for ever." Thus he piled up his transgressions and multiplied his provocations.

All this while *he was leading thousands with him in his desperate course :* both by his influence and authority he was compelling the nation to blaspheme. The whole land followed its king, save only a remnant according to the election of grace, and these bore all the fury of his wrath. The nation was prone to fall into idolatry, and willingly went with the court; when the king bade them worship Baalim, they joyfully replied "so would we have it;" and even when the most polluted emblems were set up for worship, the mass of the people greedily went after the abomina-tions. A few wept and sighed in secret, and spoke often one to another, but they had no power to alter the sad state of things, for the king was too strong for them. How sad to see a royal personage become a ringleader of iniquity! For princely example is infectious and its power for evil is boundless. Do I speak to one whose life leads others astray? Are you a man of mark? Are you placed in a position of influence? Are you a parent with children about you who will inevita-bly copy you? Are you the foreman in the workshop, or the head of a club, so that what you say and do becomes law to

feebler minds than your own? Ah, you
have the power to sin a hundred times at
once, for you make others commit the sin
in which you indulge. Your sin brings
forth many at a birth, and as by means
of mirrors the image of an object can be
multiplied, so is your sin reflected in
scores of others. The voice of your evil
life is repeated by a thousand echoes.
Think of this and beware. Why should
you destroy others as well as yourself?
Do not be guilty of the blood of your
neighbours. Do not murder your own
children's souls. Consent not to be a
jackal for the lion of the pit, or a net in
the devil's hand, for if you are such your
sin is infinite.

Nor was this all, for though it is not
recorded in the Chronicles, yet you will
find in the second book of Kings, at the
21st chapter, that *he persecuted the people
of God very furiously.* "Moreover, Manasseh shed innocent blood very much,
till he had filled Jerusalem from one end
of it to another." He was so zealous
in carrying out his idolatries that he
could not endure the sight of a man who
would not bow before his images. He
hated those ancient Nonconformists, those

Protestants, those separatists, those Puritans, and he made laws to put them down, so that the worshippers of Jehovah were "stoned and were sawn asunder, they wandered about in sheep skins and goat skins, destitute, afflicted, tormented." We cannot vouch for the tradition that the prophet Isaiah was put to death by him by being sawn in sunder, but terrible as is the legend it is not at all improbable. Manasseh had his Bartholomew Massacre and his unholy Inquisition. He was a bloody persecutor during much of his long life, and left marks of his reign of terror all over the land. Persecution is one of the most heinous of sins, and greatly provokes the Most High, for the Lord has said concerning his people, "He that toucheth you toucheth the apple of my eye." Manasseh did, as it were, thrust his finger into the eye of God. This was a heaven-provoking crime! In these days the law does not allow the shedding of innocent blood, but there are people in the world who go as far as they can in persecution. There are modes of torture which can be used against a believing wife, such as will hardly be imagined. Children can be

provoked and grievously afflicted by un-
christian parents. "Trials of cruel mock-
ings," are mentioned by the apostle, and
they are very cruel and trying too. We
have known persons use towards brothers
and sisters, and even towards children,
such threats and modes of abuse, and such
taunts and jeers, that they have made
their lives bitter as with heavy bondage.
This is against God a very high offence.
You cannot anger a man more than by
ill-using his little ones. Touch his children and you bring the colour into his
face directly, and the man's temper is
up; and he who insults, and mocks, and
grieves God's children will one day find
that the Lord will avenge his own elect
though he bear long with them.

Only one more touch to finish this dark
picture—was there ever a blacker?—and
it is this which is contained in the tenth
verse: "And the Lord spake to Manasseh, and to his people, but they would
not hearken." *Manasseh refused warning.*
He did not sin without being rebuked.
God did try the bit and bridle upon him,
but they were of no use, for this wild
horse took the bit between his teeth and
dashed on in utter madness. He could

not, he would not, bow before the loving
admonition of the Most High. This makes
sin to be exceedingly sinful, for, " He,
that being often reproved hardeneth his
neck, shall suddenly be destroyed, and that
without remedy." Without rebuke a man's
sin may be far less than it must be after
the rejection of admonitions from the
mouth of God. To stifle conscience, and
refuse loving warning is to incur fearful
guilt.

Such was this Manasseh—the very chief
of sinners. I feel certain that among
those whom I address there is not a
grosser sinner than he was, and I might
almost say there never lived a worse ; he
has an evil eminence among the lovers of
iniquity, *and yet he was saved by divine
grace!* O you who hear these words or
read them never dare to doubt the possibility of your being forgiven. If such a
wretch as Manasseh was brought to repentance, surely no one need despair.

III. Now listen to what almighty
grace, nevertheless, did for Manasseh,
whom we will now think of as A RE-
MARKABLE CONVERT. His conversion
began, or *was wrought at its commence-
ment, instrumentally, by his afflictions.*

The king of Assyria came against him,
and he was unable to resist his assault.
Sennacherib, a former king of Assyria,
had invaded the land in the days of Hezekiah, and the Lord had delivered his
people, but there was no God to deliver
Manasseh, and so the armies of Assyria
overran the land, and the royal idolater
found his idols fail him. For fear of
being captured in Jerusalem he fled and
concealed himself in a thornbrake, but
was soon captured or "taken among the
thorns," and led in chains to Babylon. He
seems to have been very severely handled
by the king, who was, probably, Esarhad-
don, king of united Assyria and Babylon,
for he is spoken of as taken with hooks,
such as large fish are taken with, or held
by a ring such as is often passed through
the noses of wild beasts. If this be only
a figure, it represents Manasseh as regarded by the Assyrian king as an un-
manageable beast to be subdued by rigour
even as a bull is managed by a ring in his
nose. We are also told that he was loaded
with double fetters of brass, and was taken
down to Babylon, to be kept in a close
dungeon. The Assyrians were notoriously
a fierce people, and Manasseh having

provoked them, felt all the degradation,
scorn, and cruelty which anger could invent.
He who had trusted idols was made a slave
to an idolatrous people ; he who had shed
blood very much was now in daily jeo-
pardy of the shedding of his own ; he who
had insulted the Lord must now be continually insulted himself. That which he
had meted out was measured into his own
bosom. He was the prodigal in actual
life, in a far country where he fain would
have filled his belly with the husks that
the swine did eat, and no man gave unto
him. While fast chained in prison, the
iron entered into his soul, and his thoughts
troubled him. How vain now to cry to
Baal or Ashtaroth. The stars that peered
through the grated bars of his dungeon
upbraided him for his foolish worship,
and the sun and moon took up the tale of
rebuke. Familiar spirits were familiar no
longer, and magic with its lying wonders
could not release him ; no, nor the witches
and wizards with their enchantments.
There he lies, and fears that there he will
lie and rot ; but in his extremity infinite
mercy visits him, and *his soul finds vent for
its misery in prayer.* " He besought the
Lord God of his fathers." I admire the

historian's words. He had dishonoured
his father as well as his God, but now he
bethinks him of his godly ancestors and
their holy faith. Surely his desire to return to his father's faith bore some like-
ness to that more spiritual resolve of the
prodigal, "I will arise and go unto my
father." It has often happened that men
have been by grace the more readily led to
God because he was their father's or their
mother's God; human love is thus dis-
solved in the nobler passion. Manasseh
thinks, meditates, considers, reviews his
life, and loathes himself; he remembers
how his father prospered by Jehovah's
aid, and perhaps also recollects the marvellous story of how Jehovah heard his
father's prayer when he was near to die,
and raised him to life again. At any
rate, in the dungeon he imitated his
father, turned his face to the wall and
wept sore and prayed. "If," said he,
"God saved my father's life, peradven-
ture he may forgive my sin and bring
me out of this horrible captivity." Thus
hopefully he cried unto the Lord. O
friend, will not you also cry unto the
God whom you have offended? Will not
you say, "God be merciful to me a

sinner?" Try, I beseech thee, the power of prayer.

But notice what went with his prayer; for, O sinner, if thou wouldst have mercy of God it must go with thine: "*he humbled himself greatly*." Ah, he had been a great man before: he was high and mighty Manasseh who would have his own way and dared defy the Lord to his face; but now he sings another song, he lies low as a penitent and begs as a sinner. How would he now use the language of his forefather David—" Have mercy upon me, O God, and blot out my transgressions." There is in the Apocrypha a book entitled " The Prayer of Manasses," which was probably composed to gratify the curiosity which would like to know how so great a transgressor prayed. Of course it is spurious, but it contains some good and humble language almost meet for the lips of so great a penitent, though far more coherent and oratorical than his words are likely to have been. What a broken prayer Manasseh's must have been, and what groans and sobs and sighs were heard and seen by the great Father of spirits, as his erring child sought his face in the gloomy cells of Babylon! Let such be your frame of mind, O sinner. Be ashamed at your sin and folly. Confess it with mourning, and abhor yourself on account of it. May the Holy Spirit bring you to this mind.

Brethren, *the Lord heard Manasseh!* Glory be to infinite grace, the Lord heard him. Bloodstained hands were lifted to heaven, and yet the Lord accepted the prayer. A heart that had been the palace of Satan, a heart which had conceived mischief and brought forth cruelty, a proud rebellious heart humbled itself before God, and the Lord pardoned and smiled upon the penitent, and, as a testimony of his infinite mercy, he moved the king of Assyria to take Manasseh out of prison and restore him to his throne. The Lord doeth great marvels, and sheweth great mercy unto the very chief of sinners. O that this might persuade some to test and try this gracious God. Manasseh had not such a clear revelation as you have; you have heard of God in Christ Jesus reconciling the world unto himself, not imputing their trespasses unto them. Let the wounds of Jesus encourage you, let his intercession for sinners cheer you. God is ready to pardon, and his bowels yearn towards you. Come even now and seek his face, ye vilest among men.

Now, can you picture Manasseh going back from Babylon attended by a cohort of Assyrian soldiery? The poor believers in Jerusalem have had a little respite while he has been in durance. Perhaps they even ventured to the temple, and restored the worship of Jehovah; at any rate, they crept out of the holes and corners in which they had laid hid, and breathed more freely. But now it is rumoured that the persecuting king is coming back—that the hunter of the souls of men is again abroad. What dread seized the minds of the timid among the godly, and how earnestly the brave-spirited steeled their hearts for the conflict. More stonings, more sawings asunder! Can it be that these horrors are to be renewed? The righteous meet and sorrowfully plead with God that he would not permit the light to be quite quenched, nor give over his people like sheep to the slaughter. What a day of foreboding it must have been when the king came through the city gates. But, perhaps, some of them watched him, and when he passed by a shrine of Baal, they noticed

that he did not bow. The image of
Ashtaroth stood in the high place, but
they observed that he turned away his
head as though he would not look in that
direction; and what was their joy when
they afterwards read his proclamation,
that, from henceforth, Judah should worship Jehovah alone. What hanging down
of the heads for the ritualistic, idolatrous
party, and what joy among the evangeli-
cals that the king himself had come over
to their side—for now the truth and the
true-hearted would have the upper hand.
What triumph was felt by the saints when
the king sent the cleansers to the temple
to pull down the carved image—the blessed
virgin, which stood in its own niche, and
to take down altar and reredos and rood
and relic, which defiled the house of the
Lord. Loud was the psalm of delight
when they saw the king standing to offer
peace offerings and thankofferings to Jehovah, and knew that henceforth there
was to be no Baal worship, no Ashtaroth
worship, no more of the obscene symbols;
for all these things were swept away.
Then went up their hymns, and they
blessed the Lord with all their hearts,
singing, " In Judah is God known : his

name is great in Israel. There brake he
the arrows of the bow, the shield, and
the sword, and the battle." O that such
songs might be sung in the church of
Christ because of some of you.

Manasseh also *did his best to undo
what he had done,* and to restore what he
had damaged; for those who are really
converted show it practically. Restitution must be made for wrong done, or
repentance is a sham. All the evil we
have done we must labour to remedy, or
our penitence is only skin deep. That
conversion which does not convert or turn
the life is no conversion at all; Manasseh's
life ran in a course directly opposite to its
former direction, for the Lord had turned
him and he was turned indeed. Glory be
to God for his mighty work in this royal
sinner's case, honour and praise be unto
the love eternal, the grace unbounded, the
power omnipotent, which changed such a
wretch, so that the fierce destroyer became
a defender of the faith and a reformer in
the house of the Lord. Can he not do the
like with you? Can he not cause you also
to be turned from the power of Satan unto
God?

One or two things remain to be said by

way of practical address. First, dear friend, *adore divine grace*. Never limit its power, but believe it able to convert the most abandoned; believe that it can save you. Since our Lord Jesus ever liveth to intercede for those who come unto God by him, he is able also to save them unto the uttermost. You cannot have too large ideas of divine grace, for where sin abounded grace does much more abound.

But, secondly, *never turn it into an excuse for continuing in sin*, for this case of Manasseh, with all its mercy, is still a sad one. Though we have seen how grace gave it a good ending, yet, take it for all in all, it is a sad case, and as a life Manasseh's was wasted, misspent, and full of wretchedness. Although he sought to mend matters, he could not fully undo what he had done. The people were nothing like as eager to follow the right as they were the wrong; and after many years of royal patronage of idolatry it was not easy for the masses to turn round on a sudden, and so the people sacrificed on their high places, though only to Jehovah, and their hearts went after their idols still. The polluting idolatries had degraded the people ; licentiousness had taken possession of them, and from this evil there was no drawing them back. Indeed, their sin was so great that God resolved that the sin of Judah under Manasseh should never be forgiven, and it never was. A respite was given, for Josiah reigned a little time, but it was God's mind and purpose that the sin should never be put away. If you read in the twenty-third chapter of the Second Book of Kings, and the twenty-sixth verse, you will see that though Manasseh himself was saved as a penitent yet the transgression of Judah in having followed him in all that sin still remained. "Notwithstanding, the Lord turned not from the fierceness of his great wrath, wherewith his anger was kindled against Judah, because of all the provocations that Manasseh had provoked him withal." And so in the twenty-fourth, at the third verse, "Surely, at the commandment of the Lord came this upon Judah, to remove them out of his sight, for the sins of Manasseh, according to all that he shed (for he filled Jerusalem with innocent blood), which the Lord would not pardon." So, though a man may be pardoned, yet he may have been the occasion of sin in others, which never will be blotted out. How strange is this! A man may lead others into such evil that in it they will abide and perish, although through mighty grace he may himself be forgiven. Will any of you venture upon such a hazardous business? Even if you knew that your own house would be saved, would you burn other men's houses? Would you wish to be the cause of other men's ruin even if you were sure that in the end you would repent? No, be not so base. Lay hold on Jesus and eternal life even now, that you may not have a misspent life to mourn over.

Note well that Manasseh after death had no honour. It does not say of him as of Hezekiah, that they buried him in the sepulchres of the kings, but they buried him in the palace garden. As Matthew Henry very well says, " A pardoned sinner may get back his comfort, but he can never get back his credit." It is hard to live an ill life for years, and yet die in honourable repute, because of late repentance. Even if grace comes in to make the conclusion of your career to be bright with salvation, it is an awful thing to have led a life which, taken as a whole, is rather a curse to mankind than a blessing. So when I tell you what divine grace can do, do not continue in sin to try that grace. You have sinned enough already. Do pray God to do more for you than for Manasseh,—namely, save you from Manasseh's sins, and make you to lead a life which from this moment to its end shall glow with the grace of God. How much better to live like Josiah than like Manasseh ! Who would not infinitely prefer to lead the life of Moses, perpetually serving God, than that of a hoary sinner who is saved at the last " so as by fire."

The last word is, *seek for mercy, all of you:* do not neglect it because of its greatness, but the rather hasten to receive it. Since we all need more mercy than we imagine, let us cry for it at once in hearty earnest. Let us come to the fountain which is opened for the house of David and for the inhabitants of Jerusalem, and wash therein. Let us, by faith in Jesus' blood, wash and be clean. The Lord make us to do so, for Jesus' sake. Amen.

# THE
# WOMAN THAT WAS A SINNER,
## OR,
# THE LOVING PENITENT

"And, behold, a woman in the city, which was a sinner, when she knew that Jesus sat at meat in the Pharisee's house, brought an alabaster box of ointment, and stood at his feet behind him weeping, and began to wash his feet with tears, and did wipe them with the hairs of her head, and kissed his feet, and anointed them with the ointment."
—Luke vii. 37, 38.

MANASSEH'S case gave us an opportunity of dwelling upon the dark side of conversion: we saw in him the darkness from which a man needs to be turned, and how grace is able to turn him. The Scripture has presented his lost estate with remarkable fulness, and therefore we have dwelt upon it at considerable length, our hope being that some far-gone rebel would take encouragement from it to seek the Lord. If any man tested the longsuffering of God to the utmost degree it was surely Manasseh, yet that longsuffering held out and worked his salvation. May some of the chief of sinners see in this the needlessness and folly of despair, and take heart of hope that the Lord will pardon them also.

In the case of " the woman that was a sinner," details of her sin are very scanty, as is natural in a book so delicate and tender as the New Testament; but we have quite a narrative of her penitence and its fruits, and in these she shines resplendently as a wonder of grace. We have seen enough of the disease in Manasseh, let us see the cure in this loving woman. The wayward king shows us the stone in the rough, in the woman we shall see it polished after the similitude of a palace. Manasseh reveals the lion in the unrenewed nature, and the woman shows us the lion tamed into a lamb. Our last subject taught us to lament the depravity engendered by the fall, our present will lead us to rejoice in the restoration wrought by redemption.

We will consider the life of this famous penitent under three heads, and notice, first, *her former character;* then, *her deed of love which showed her new character;* and, thirdly, *our Lord's treatment of her.*

I.   Let us very briefly look at THE WOMAN'S CHARACTER, to begin with, in order that we may see the horrible pit out of which she was taken.

We do not know much about her. Romish expositors generally insist upon it that she was Mary Magdalene, but this appears to other writers to have been quite impossible.   Certainly it does not seem probable that a woman possessed with seven devils should follow the trade of "a sinner."   Demoniacal possession was akin to madness, and it was frequently accompanied by epilepsy, and one would think that Magdalene was more fit to be a patient at an infirmary than an inmate of a reformatory.   Some have even been so mistaken as to suppose this woman to have been Mary of Bethany, but this will never do.   One cannot associate with the lovely household of Martha and Mary the horrible course of pollution implied in the vice which earned for this woman the special name of a "sinner."   Besides, although both women anointed our Lord, yet the place, the time, the manner were all different. I need not stay to show you the difference, for that is not the point in hand.

This woman was distinguished by the title of "*a sinner*," and her touch was regarded by Simon the Pharisee as defiling. We are all sinners, but she was a sinner by profession, sin was her occupation, and probably her livelihood. The name in her case had an emphatic sense which involved shame, and dishonour of the worst kind. The city streets wherein she dwelt could have told you how well she deserved her name. Poor fallen daughter of Eve, she had forsaken the guide of her youth, and forgotten the covenant of her God. She was one of those against whom Solomon warns young men, saying, "Her house inclineth unto death, and her paths unto the dead." Yet as Rahab was saved by faith, even so was she, for grace covereth even a harlot's sins.

She was *a well-known sinner:* ill fame had branded her, so that Simon the Pharisee recognised her as one of the town's unhallowed sisterhood. Her way of life was common town talk; persons of decent character would not associate with her, she was cut off from respectable society, and, like a leper, put outside the camp of social life. She was a sinner marked and labelled: there was no mistaking her, infamy had set its seal upon her.

She was one who had evidently *gone a great way in sin*, because our Saviour, who was far from being prejudiced against her, as Simon was, and never uttered a word that would exaggerate the evil in any one, yet spake of "her sins which are many." She loved much, for much had been forgiven ; she was the five hundred pence debtor as compared with Simon, who owed but fifty. It is not difficult to imagine her unhappy story, because that story is so commonly repeated around us. We know not how she was at first led into evil ways. Perhaps her trustful heart was deceived by flattering words and promises ; perhaps the treachery of one too dearly loved led her into sin, and afterwards deserted her to loneliness and shame. Perhaps her mother's heart was broken, and her father's head was bowed down with sorrow ; but she became bold enough to pursue the sin into which she had at first been betrayed, and became the decoyer of others. That long hair of hers, I fear, is rightly called by Bishop Hall "the net which she was wont to spread to catch her amorous companions." She was a sinner of the city in which she dwelt, and though her name is not mentioned, it was far too well known in her own day. She had lived an evil life we know not how long, but, certainly, she had greatly sinned, for her own flowing tears as well as the Saviour's estimate of her life prove that she had been no ordinary offender. Let equal sinners be encouraged to go to Jesus as she did.

But *all her sin was known to Jesus.* I mention this, not at all as a fact you do not know, but as one which any trembling sinner may do well to remember. If you have fallen into the same vice in a greater or less degree, whether others know it or not, Jesus knows all about it. Our Lord allowed her to wash his feet with her tears, but he knew well what those eyes had looked upon. When he allowed those lips to kiss his feet he knew right well what language those lips had used in years gone by; and when he suffered her to show her love to him he knew how foul her heart had aforetime been with every unhallowed desire. Her

lustful imaginations and unchaste desires,
her wanton words and shameless acts were
all before the Saviour's mind far more
vividly than they were before her own,
for she had forgotten much; but he
knew all. With all her tender sense of
sin, she herself did not apprehend all the
heinousness of her guilt as the perfect
mind of Jesus did : and yet though she
was a sinner, a well-known sinner, and
known best of all to the Saviour to be such,
yet, glory be to divine grace, she was not
cast out when she came to Jesus, but she
obtained mercy, and is now shining in
heaven as a bright and special star to the
glory of the love of Christ.

When this woman stood in the house of
Simon she was *a believing sinner*. We do
not know how she became a convert, but
according to the harmony of the gospels
this particular incident fits in just after
Matt. xi. ; that is to say, if Luke has
written his story with the intent of chro-
nological correctness—and if the harmo-
nies are right, this passage comes in after
the following blessed word, " Come unto
me all ye that labour and are heavy
laden, and I will give you rest : take my
yoke upon you and learn of me, for I

am meek and lowly of heart, and ye
shall find rest unto your souls, for my
yoke is easy and my burden is light." Did
this woman hear this gracious invitation? Did she feel that she was labouring and heavy laden? Did she look into
the face of the great Teacher and feel that
he spake the truth, and did she come to
him and find rest? Doubtless her faith
came by hearing: did she hear in some
crowd in the street the sweet wooing voice
of the Sinner's Friend? Was this the
means of making " the woman that was a
sinner " into the woman that anointed
Jesus' feet? We are not informed as to
the particular means, nor is it of any con-
sequence. She was converted, and that is
enough; how it came about is a small
matter. Perhaps even she herself could
not have told us the precise words which
impressed her mind, for many are most
assuredly brought to Jesus, but the work
has been so gentle, gradual, and gracious
that they feel themselves renewed; but
hardly know how it came about. On the
other hand, from the marked change in
her character it is highly probable that
she did know the day and the hour and
the precise means : and if so, dear were

the words which called her from the ways
of folly, sin, and shame. I do not suppose
that our Saviour had, at that time, delivered the memorable parable of the
prodigal son, but it may have been
some similar discourse which won her
attention, when she made one of a crowd
of publicans and sinners who drew near to
hear the Lord Jesus. Pressing forward
among the men to catch those silver tones,
so full of music, she wondered at the
man whose face was so strangely beautiful, and yet so marvellously sad, whose
eyes were so bright with tears, and whose
face so beamed with love and earnest-
ness. The very look of that mirror of
love may have affected her, a glance at
that holy countenance may have awed
her, and his tones of deep pity and tender
warning—all these held her fast, and drew
her to abhor her sin and accept the joyful
message which the great Teacher had come
to proclaim. She believed in Jesus, she was
saved, and therefore she loved her Saviour.

When she came to the Pharisee's house
she was *a forgiven sinner*. She carried an
alabaster box in her hand with which to
anoint him, because she felt that he had
been a priest to her and had cleansed her.

She brought her choicest treasure to give
to him because he had bestowed on her
the choicest of all gifts, namely, the forgiveness of sin. She washed his feet because he had washed her soul, she wept
because she believed, and loved because
she trusted. She was, when she entered
the room, in a condition of rest as to her
forgiveness, for men are seldom deeply
grateful for mercies which they are not
sure of having obtained. Though after
that deed she rose a step higher, and became fully assured of her acceptance, even
at her first coming she was conscious of
forgiven sin, and for that reason she paid
her vows unto the forgiving Lord, whom
her soul loved.

Our text begins with a "behold"; and
it may well be so, for a forgiven sinner is a
wonder to heaven, and earth, and hell. A
forgiven sinner! Though God has made
this round world exceeding fair, yet no
work of creation reflects so much of his
highest glory as the manifestation of his
grace in a pardoned sinner. If you range
all the stars around, and if it be so that
every star is filled with a race of intelligent beings, yet, methinks, among unfallen
existences there can be no such marvel as

a forgiven sinner. At any rate he is a wonder to himself, and he will never cease admiring the grace which pardoned and accepted him. What a miracle to herself must this woman have been. For a case like hers she had seen no precedent, and this must have made it the more surprising to her : when your case also appears to stand out by itself alone as a towering peak of grace, refrain not from wondering and causing others to wonder. "All glory to God," may some say, "I whose name could not be mentioned without making the cheek of modesty to crimson, *I* am washed in the blood of the Lamb ! I who was a blasphemer, who sat on the drunkard's bench, who gloried in being an infidel, and denied the God-head of Christ, I, even I, am saved from wrath through him. I who played a dishonest part, who respected not the laws of man any more than those of God, I who went to an excess of riot, even I am made whiter than snow through faith in Christ Jesus.

> 'Tell it unto sinners, tell,
> I am, I am saved from hell.' "

Let all know it upon earth, and let heaven know it, and let the loud harps ring in yon celestial halls, because of matchless grace.

Behold, then, this woman's character; and, remember, however fallen you may have been, the grace of God can yet save you.

II. Now, secondly, let us consider, at some length, THE DEED OF LOVE WHICH INDICATED HER CONVERSION. Her conduct as a convert was wide as the poles asunder from that of her unregenerate state : she became as evidently a penitent as she had been a sinner. One of the expositors upon this passage says that he cannot so much expound it as weep over it ; and I think every Christian must feel very much in that humour. O that our eyes were as ready with tears of repentance as hers were ! O that our hearts were as full of love as hers, and our hands as ready to serve the forgiving Lord. If she has exceeded some of us in the publicity of her sin, yet has she not exceeded all of us in the fervency of her affection ?

Let us notice what she did, and the first of twelve matters to which I shall call your attention is *the earnest interest which she took in the Lord Jesus.* "Behold, a woman in the city, which was a sinner, when she knew that Jesus sat at meat." She had a quick ear for anything about Jesus. When she heard the news it did not pass in at one ear and out at the other, but she was interested in the information, and straightway went to the Pharisee's house to find him. There were hundreds in that city who did not care a farthing where Jesus was. If they heard the general gossip about him it did not concern them in the least, he was nothing to them; but when *she* knew it, she was in motion at once to come even to his feet. Jesus never again will be an object of indifference to a forgiven sinner. If the Lord has pardoned you, you will henceforth feel the deepest interest in your Saviour, and in all things which concern his kingdom and work among men. Now, if you have to remove to any place you will want to know first—"Where can I hear the gospel? Are there any lovers of Jesus there?" If you are informed about a town or country, the information will not be complete till you have enquired, "How is the cause of God prospering there?" As you look upon your fellow men the thought will strike you, "How do they stand towards Christ?" When

you attend a place of worship it will not
matter much to you whether the edifice is
architecturally beautiful, or the preacher a
learned man, and a great orator, you want
to know whether you can hear of Jesus
in that place, and be likely to meet with
him in that assembly. Your cry will be,
" Tell me, O thou whom my soul loveth,
where thou feedest?" If you perceive a sweet
savour of Christ in the place, you feel that
you have had a good Sabbath-day ; but
if Jesus Christ be wanting, you consider
everything to be wanting, and you groan
over a lost Sabbath. A soul that has
tasted Christ's love cannot be put off
with anything short of him, it hungers
and thirsts after him, and any good word
about him is sweet unto the taste. Is it
so with you ?

Notice, next, *the readiness of her mind
to think of something to be done for Jesus.*
" When she knew that Jesus sat at meat
in the Pharisee's house she brought an
alabaster box of ointment "—she was
quick and ready in her thoughts of service. She would not appear before the
Lord empty, but the resolve to bring an
offering, and the selection of that offering,
were quickly made. She would get that

alabaster box of aromatic balsam, the daintiest and costliest perfume that she had, and she would anoint his feet to do him honour. Many minds are inventive for the things of the world, but they seem to have no quickness of thought in reference to the service of Christ : they proceed with dull routine, but never flash out with spontaneous deeds of love. This woman showed an original genius in her love, she was no copier of a former example, her plan of service had the dew of freshness upon it. Mary of Bethany did something like it, but that was afterwards : this was the woman's own original idea. Her thoughtful soul struck out this new path for itself. It is a great thing for Christian people to carry on works commenced by others, for what should we do if the established agencies of the church should come to a standstill ? But it is pleasant to see quick wits and thoughtful faculties exercising themselves for Jesus and devising means to serve him. It is well, for instance, when a beloved sister is so fired with the love of Jesus that she feels—" I am somewhat different from other women, both in character and past experience, and I have peculiarities of gifts and disposition, therefore I will let my soul follow the bent of her gracious inclination, and I will give myself to work which is unusual in the church, but which will be specially suitable for me." Oh, for more of that voluntary service which, so far from requiring to be urged, does not even need to be instructed, but shows a sacred suggestiveness and affection which supplies the place of teaching and example. We need more contriving, inventing, and planning for Christ. See how we act towards those we love: we consider what will please them, and plot and plan some pleasant surprise for them. We put our heads together and ask— "What shall it be? Let us think of something new and off the common." That thoughtfulness is half the beauty of the act. I wish that loving believers would lay their heads together and say, "What shall be done unto him whom the Lord delighteth to honour? What shall we do for Jesus our Redeemer? What could we do best, and what is most needed to be done just now?" For, you see, this woman did the most fitting thing that could be done. Simon had not washed his feet,

it was most proper that *she* should wash
them: Simon had not kissed him, but
somebody should do so, for he deserved
every honour, and therefore she did it.
Simon had not poured oil upon his head,
or shown him any token of respect;
but her warm heart, by the Holy Spirit,
who is the creator and fosterer of all love,
devised and carried out the right thing
at the right time, as earnest believers
always do when they are willing to give
full liberty to the warm dictates of their
loving hearts.   Note that.

Notice, thirdly, *her promptness of action.*
She did not merely think that she had an
alabaster box to give, but she took it at
once, and hastened to pour out its contents.   Dear friend, you have been saved
by grace, and you have an alabaster box
upstairs which you have long meant to
bring down, but it is there still.   Half-a-
dozen times or more, when you have had
your heart warmed by the love of Christ,
you have felt that now was the time to
bring out the box, but it remains sealed
up still.   You were so pleased with yourself for having such earnest feelings and
generous resolutions that you stopped to
admire yourself, and forgot to carry out

your resolutions. You have done nothing,
though you have intended a great deal.
Do you not sometimes feel as self-contented
as if you had done something wonderful
when, after all, you have only mapped
out what you think you may possibly do
at some future time? Indeed, it is a
mighty easy thing to make yourself believe that you have really done what you
have only dreamed about. This is
wretched child's play, and the woman
before us would have none of it. She
saw the occasion and she seized it. Jesus
might not be in her city again, and she
might not be able to find him for many a
day. The thought struck her, and she
struck the thought while yet the iron was
hot, and she fashioned it into a fact.
It is usually true that second thoughts
are best, but it is not so in the service of
our Lord. The first suggestions of love,
like the first beams of the morning, are
not to be excelled for beauty and freshness. Good things had better be done at
once, without a second thought. "I con-
sulted not with flesh and blood," said the
apostle. Is it a right thing? Is it for
Jesus? Why, then, do it. Get it done
first, and even then do not think of it, but

go on to something yet beyond. In this sacred work "he gives twice who gives quickly." Promptness of action is the bloom upon the fruit which delay would brush off. What grace had the Lord given to this poor fallen woman! She shames the best of us.

Observe, in the fourth place, *her courage*. She knew that Jesus was at meat in the Pharisee's house, and she soon found him reclining, in the oriental fashion, with his feet near the door, for Simon was so uncivil that he was sure to give him a poor place at the table. Seeing the Lord, she ventured in. It needed no small bravery for her to enter the house of a Pharisee, who above all things dreaded to be touched by such a character. In her bad times she had seen the holy man gather up his garments, and leave her a broad space on the streets for fear that she should pollute his sacred person. She must have felt, as all penitent sinners do, an inward shrinking from the cold, hard, self-righteous professor of purity. She would have gone anywhere in that city rather than into Simon's house. It must have cost her a great struggle to face his frowns and severe remarks. Perhaps, however, I am wrong; indeed, I think I am, for she was so full of the desire to show her love and to honour the Lord Jesus that she forgot the Pharisee. Ay, and if the devil had been there instead of Simon, she would have dared him in his den to reach her Lord. Still there was much courage needed for one so lowly in her penitence to be able to bear the cold contemptuous look of the master of the house. Conscious that she had been a cast-away from society, yet she courageously fulfilled her mission, fearless of cruel remarks and taunting charges. O poor timid seeking soul, the Lord can give to thee also the courage of a lion in his cause, though now thou art timid as a hare.

When, then, the penitent had reached the Master's feet, note well how one grace balanced another, and observe *her humility* tempering her courage. Her boldness was not forwardness nor indelicate impertinence; no, she was as bashful as she was brave. She did not advance to our Lord's head, or thrust herself where he would readily see her, much less did she presume to address him, but she stood at his feet behind him, weeping. She was probably but a little way in the room, she courted no observation; she was near Jesus, but it was near his feet, and weeping there. To weep at his feet was honour high enough for her; she sought no uppermost seat at the banquet. Ah, dear friends, it is a blessed thing to see young converts bold, but it is equally delightful to see them humble, and they are none the worse for being very retiring if they have been great sinners.

I have been very sorry when I have seen a lack of modesty where it ought to have superabounded. There is more grace in a blush than in a brazen forehead, far more propriety in holy shamefacedness than in pious impudence. Good Bishop Hall says, "How well is the case altered! She had wont to look boldly in the face of her lovers, and now she dares not behold the awful countenance of her Saviour. She had been accustomed to send alluring beams forth into the eyes of her paramours, but now she casts dejected eyes to the earth, and dares not so much as raise them up to see those eyes from which she desired commiseration." Lowliness goes well with penitence. One would not wish humility to be corrupted into cowardice, nor courage to be poisoned

into pride.  This repenting sinner had
both excellences in proper proportion, and
the two together put her exactly in the
place where a woman that was a sinner
ought to be when saved by grace.

We see before us our reclaimed sister
looking down upon the Lord's blessed
feet, and as we mark her flowing tears we
pause to speak of *her contrition.*  She gazed
upon our Lord's feet, and I wonder
whether that sight suggested to her how
her feet had wandered and how travel-
worn had become the feet of the Lord,
who had sought and found her.

> " She knew not of the bitter way
> Those sacred feet had yet to tread,
> Nor how the nails would pierce one day
> Where now her costly balms were shed."

But she saw those feet to be all unwashed,
for Jesus had been neglected where he
ought to have been honoured ; and she saw
therein the memory of her own neglects
of him who had so freely loved her soul.
She wept at the memory of her sins, but
she wept over *his* feet ; she grieved most
because she had grieved him.  She wept
because she had sinned so much, and
then wept because he had forgiven her
so freely.  Love and grief in equal

measures made up those precious tears.
The divine Spirit was at work within
her dissolving her very soul, even as it is
written, "He causeth his wind to blow,
and the waters flow"; and again, "He
smote the rock, and the waters gushed
out." Do you marvel that she stood and
wept? Thinking of herself, and then
thinking of him, the two thoughts together were far too much for her, and what
could she do but both relieve her heart
and express it in a shower of tears?
Wherever there is a real forgiveness of
sin there will be real sorrow on account of
it. He who knows that his sin is pardoned is the man who most acceptably
exercises repentance. Our hymn puts it
on the right footing when it points, not to
the horrors of hell, but to the griefs of
Immanuel, by which our pardon is certified
to us as the deep source of sorrow for sin.

> " My sins, my sins, my Saviour,
>     How sad on thee they fall !
> Seen through thy gentle patience
>     I tenfold feel them all.
> I know they are forgiven,
>     But all their pain to me
> Is all the grief and anguish
>     They laid, my Lord, on thee."

After admiring this woman's contrition, notice *her love*. The Holy Spirit took delight in adorning her with all the graces, and she came behind in nothing, but she excelled in love. Our Lord Jesus Christ when he translated her act of anointing his feet, expressed it in the one word "love": he said, "she loved much." I cannot speak much with you concerning love, for it is rather to be felt than to be described. Words have no power to bear the weight of meaning which lies in love to Christ. O how she loved! Her eyes, her hair, her tears, herself, she counted all as nothing for his dear sake: words failed her as they fail us, and therefore she betook herself to deeds in order to let her heart have vent. Alabaster box and ointment were all too little for him, the essence of her heart was distilled to bathe his feet, and the glory of her head was unbound to furnish him with a towel. He was her Lord, her all in all: if she could have laid kingdoms at his feet she would have rejoiced to do so; as it was, she did her best, and he accepted it.

This love of hers led her to *personal service*. Her hand was the servant of her heart, and did its part in the expression of her affection.  She did not send the alabaster box to Jesus by her sister, or ask a disciple to pass it to him, but she performed the anointing with her own hand, the washing with her own tears, and the wiping with her own hair.  Love cannot be put off with proxy service ; she seeks no substitute, but offers her own person. I grant, dear brothers and sisters, that we can serve the Lord a great deal by helping others to serve him, and it is right and proper to help those who are able to labour better and more widely than we can ; but still it is not meet that we should rest content with that, we ought to be ambitious to render tribute to our Lord with our own hands.  We cannot deny ourselves the pleasure of doing some little thing for our well-beloved Lord.  Suppose this loving woman had had a sister who loved the Master even as she did, and suppose like a loving sister she had said to her, " I fear it will be too heavy a task for you to face cold-hearted Simon, I will take the box and anoint our blessed Lord, and tell him that I did it for you, and so he shall know your love."  Do you think she would have consented to the proposal ?  Ah, no, it would not have answered the purpose at all. Love refuses sponsors. She must anoint those blessed feet *herself*. Now, dear friends, you who hope that you have been forgiven, are you doing anything for Jesus? Are you in your own person serving him? If not, let me tell you, you are missing one of the greatest delights that your souls can ever know, and, at the same time, you are omitting one of the chief fruits of the Spirit. "Simon, son of Jonas, lovest thou me?" is the question, and if you wish to answer it with proof positive, then go and with your own hands feed the Saviour's sheep. Surely you cannot love him as you should unless each day has its deed of love, its sacrifice of gratitude.

Observe, next, that *her service was rendered to the Lord himself*. Read the passage and place an emphasis upon the words which refer to the Lord: "She stood at *his* feet, behind *him*, weeping, and began to wash *his* feet, and did wipe *them* with the hairs of her head, and kissed *his* feet, and anointed *them* with the ointment." It was not for Peter and James and John that she acted as servitor. I have no doubt she would have done anything for any of his disciples, but at this time all her thoughts were with her Lord, and all her desire was to honour *him*. It is a delightful thing for Christian people to lay themselves out distinctly for the Lord Jesus. There should be more ministering unto him, more definite aiming at his glory. To give money to the poor is good, but sometimes it is better to spend it upon Jesus more distinctly, even though some Judas or other should complain of waste.

> " Love is the true economist,
>   She breaks the box and gives her all ;
>   Yet not one precious drop is miss'd,
>   Since on *his* head and feet they fall."

One is glad to serve the church ; who would not wait upon the bride for the bride-groom's sake ? One is glad to go into the streets and lanes of the city to gather in poor sinners, but our main motive is to honour the Saviour. See, then, how she who was once a harlot has become a zealous lover of the Lord, and is ready to wash her Lord's feet, or perform any service which may be permitted her, if so be she may work a good work upon him.

Further, remark, that what she did she did very *earnestly*. She washed his feet, but it was with tears ; she wiped them, but it was with those luxurious tresses which were all unbound and dishevelled, that she might make a towel of them for his blessed feet. She kissed his feet, and she did it again and again, for she did not cease to kiss his feet, or if she made a moment's pause, it was only that she might pour on more of the balsam. She was altogether taken up with her Lord and his work ; her entire nature concurred in what she did, and aroused itself to do it well. True love is intense, its coals burn with vehement heat, it makes all things around it living. Dead services cannot be endured by living hearts. I know some people, I hope they are Christian people, but they belong to the cold-blooded animals, you never perceive the smallest warmth in them ; they are patent refrigerators, walking masses of ice. If you shake hands with them, you think you have got a dead fish in your hand, there is nothing hearty and warm about them. If such people speak about Jesus Christ, it is in the coolest possible terms. If they preach, their sermons are best appreciated on a hot summer's day, when you need something cool and airy : but the man who feels he has been forgiven

much, and owes much to the Saviour,
throws his whole heart into what he has
to say for him.  Give me a woman that
is full of love to Jesus, and you shall see
how she will labour in the Redeemer's
service.  I have heard of a preacher who
was so intensely earnest that, when one
complained of his sermon being short, an
old farmer replied, " Short, yes, but look
at the weight of it.  Every word he spoke
weighed half-a-hundredweight."  I like a
preacher of that kind who is so full of
love that every word is a power.  Everything we do for Jesus should be done intensely, earnestly, vehemently.  To keep
back part of the price from him would be
shameful, to be neither cold nor hot would
be fatal, to be consumed with zeal for him
is no more than his due.  To do no more
than you feel obliged to do, and that in
about as slovenly a style as you well can
—this is a poor, dead way of living, unworthy of a soul redeemed of blood.  He
who loves much cannot endure a sleepy
religion : he devotes himself to the Lord
Jesus with all his heart.

Furthermore, notice the woman's *ab-
sorption in her work*.  There she stood
anointing his feet with ointment and

kissing them again and again. Simon
shook his head, but what of that? He
frowned and cast black looks at her, but
she ceased not to wash his feet with her
tears. She was too much occupied with
her Lord to care for scowling Pharisees.
Whether any one observed her or not, or
whether observers approved or censured,
was a very small matter to her, she went
quietly on, accomplishing the suggestion
of her loving heart.

And *what she did was so real, so practical,* so free from the mere froth of profession and pretence. She never *said* a
word : and why not? Because it was all
act and all heart with her. Words !
Some abound in them, but what wretched
things words are wherewith to express a
heart. As in a glass darkly can we see
the reflection of a soul's love in its most
passionate utterances. Actions are far
more loud-voiced and have a sweeter
tone than words. This woman had done
with speech, for the time being, at any
rate, and tears and dishevelled hair,
and poured-out balsam must speak for
her. She was too much in earnest to
call anyone's attention to what she was
doing, or to care for anyone's opinion,

much less to court commendation, or
to answer the ugly looks of the proud
professor who scorned her. This tho-
rough oblivion of all except her Lord
constituted in a measure the charm of
her deed of love; it was whole-hearted
and entire loyalty which her homage revealed. Now, dearly beloved in the Lord
Jesus Christ, I do pray that you and I, as
pardoned sinners, may be so taken up
with the service of our Lord Jesus Christ
that it may not matter to us who smiles
or who frowns; and may we never take
the trouble to defend ourselves if people
find fault, or even wish for anybody to
commend us, but be so taken up with
*him* and the work he has given us to do,
and with the love we feel to *him*, that we
know nothing else. If all others run
away from the work, if all discourage us,
or if they all praise us, may we take but
small notice of them, but keep steadily to
our loving service of Jesus. If grace
enables us to do this it will be greatly
magnified.

See, dear friends, what grace made of
" the woman that was a sinner." Perhaps
you thought her worse than yourselves in
her carnal estate, what think you when

you see her as a penitent? What think
ye of yourselves if you stand side by side
with her? Do you not blush for very
shame, and ask for forgiveness of your
Lord for the slenderness of your affection?

III.  Lastly, let us see THE SAVIOUR'S
BEHAVIOUR TO HER. What did he do?

First, *he silently accepted her service.*
He did not move his feet away, did not
rebuke her, or bid her begone.  He knew
that reflections were being cast upon his
character by his allowing her to touch
him, yet he did not forbid her, but, on
the contrary, continued quietly enjoying
the feast of repentance, gratitude, and
love, which she spread for him.  He was
refreshed by seeing such grace in one who
had aforetime been so far from God.  The
perfumed balsam was not so grateful to
his feet as her love was to his soul, for
Jesus delights in love, especially in penitent love.  Her tears did not fall in vain,
they refreshed the heart of Jesus, who
delights in the tears of repentance.  The
applause of a nation would not have solaced
him one half so much as this woman's
pure, grateful, contrite, humble love.  His
silence gave consent, yea, even approbation,
and she was happy enough to be allowed

to indulge herself in expressions of adoring affection.

Then **the Lord** went a little farther. He turned round and *looked at her,* and said to Simon, " Seest thou this woman ?" That glance of his must have encouraged her, and made her heart dance for joy. As soon as ever that eye of his lighted on her she could see that all was right ; she knew that, whoever frowned, there were no frowns on that brow, and she was filled with supreme content.

Next, *the Lord spoke, and defended her triumphantly,* and praised her for her deed : yes, and he went beyond that, and *personally spoke to her,* and said, " Thy sins be forgiven thee," setting a seal to the pardon which she had received, and making her assurance doubly sure. This was a joy worth worlds.

> " Oh might I hear thy heavenly tongue
>   But whisper, ' Thou art mine' ;
> That heavenly word should raise my song
>   To notes almost divine."

She had a choice blessing in hearing from his own lips that her faith was firmly based, and that she was indeed forgiven. Then she received a direction from him as

to what to do—"Go in peace." A forgiven sinner is anxious to know what he
may do to please his Lord. "Show me
what thou wouldst have me to do," was
Paul's prayer. So our Lord Jesus seemed
to say, "Beloved, do not stop here battling
with these Pharisees. Do not tarry in
this crowd of cavillers. Go home in perfect peace; and as you have made home
unhappy by your sin, make it holy by
your example." That is just, I think,
what the Lord Jesus would have me say
to my dear friends who have followed me
in this discourse. You see what grace
can do, go home and let your family see
it. If any of you are conscious of great
sin, and have received great forgiveness,
and therefore wish to show your love to
Jesus, do what is on your heart, but at
the same time remember that he would
have you go in peace. Let a holy calm
abide in your breasts. Do not enter into
the vain janglings and endless contro-
versies of the hour. Do not worry yourself with the battles of the newspapers and
magazines that are everlastingly worrying
poor souls with modern notions. Go in
peace. You know what you do know; keep
to that. You know your sin, and you know

Christ your Saviour; keep to him, and live for him. Go home into the family circle, and do there everything you can to make home happy, and to bring your brothers and sisters to Christ, and to encourage your father and mother, if they have not yet found the Saviour.

Home is especially a woman's sphere. There she reigns as a queen: let her reign well. Around the hearth and at the table, in the sweets of domestic relationships and quiet friendships, a woman will do more for the glory of the Lord Jesus Christ than by getting up to preach. In the cases of men also, many who long to flash in public had better by far shine at home. Go home in peace, and by a happy, holy life, show to others what saints God can make out of sinners. You have seen what sin and the devil can do to degrade, go and prove what grace and the Holy Spirit can do to elevate, and may many, cheered by your example, come and trust your Lord.

# THE DYING THIEF;

## OR,

## THE LONE WITNESS.

"And one of the malefactors which were hanged railed on him, saying, If thou be Christ, save thyself and us. But the other answering rebuked him, saying, Dost not thou fear God, seeing thou art in the same condemnation? And we indeed justly; for we receive the due reward of our deeds: but this man hath done nothing amiss. And he said unto Jesus, Lord, remember me when thou comest into thy kingdom. And Jesus said unto him, Verily I say unto thee, To-day shalt thou be with me in Paradise." Luke xxiii. 39—43.

THE dying thief was certainly a very great wonder of grace. He has generally been looked upon from one point of view only, as a sinner called at the eleventh hour, and therefore an instance of special mercy because he was so near to die. Enough has been made of that circumstance by others: to my mind it is by no means the most important point in the narrative.

Had the thief been predestined to come down from the cross and live for half a century longer his conversion would have been neither more nor less than it was. The work of grace which enabled him to die in peace would, if it had been the Lord's will, have enabled him to live in holiness. We may well admire divine grace when it so speedily makes a man fit for the bliss of heaven, but it is equally to be adored when it makes him ready for the battle of earth. To bear a saved sinner away from all further conflict is great grace; but the power and love of God are, if anything, even more conspicuous when like a sheep surrounded by wolves, or a spark in the midst of the sea, a believer is enabled to live on in the teeth of an ungodly world and maintain his integrity to the end. Dear friend, whether you die as soon as you are born again, or remain on earth for many years, is comparatively a small matter, and will not materially alter your indebtedness to divine grace. In the one case the great Husbandman will show how he can bring his flowers speedily to perfection; and in the other he will prove how he can preserve them in blooming beauty despite the frosts and snows of earth's cruel winter : in either case your experience will reveal the same love and power.

There are other things, it seems to me, to be seen in the conversion of the thief besides the one single matter of his being brought to know the Lord when near to death's door.

Observe the singular fact that our Lord Jesus Christ should die in the company of two malefactors. It was probably planned in order to bring him shame, and it was regarded by those who cried, "Crucify him ! crucify him !" as an additional ignominy. Their malice decreed that he should die *as* a criminal, and *with* criminals, and in the centre, between two, to show that they thought him the worst of the three ; but God in his own way baffled the malice of the foe, and turned it to the triumph and glory of his dear Son ; for, had there been no dying thief hanging at his side, then one of the most illustrious trophies of his love would not have been gained, and we should not have been able to sing to his praise—

> " The dying thief rejoiced to see
> That fountain in his day ;
> And there have I, though vile as he,
> Washed all my sins away !"

His enemies gave our Lord Jesus an opportunity for still continuing the seeking as well as the saving of the lost. They found him an occasion for manifesting his conquering grace when they supposed they were heaping scorn upon him. How truly did the prophet in the psalm say— "He that sitteth in the heavens shall laugh, the Lord shall have them in derision;" for that which was meant to increase his misery revealed his majesty. Moreover, though it was intended to add an ingredient of bitterness to his cup, I do not doubt that it supplied him with a draught of comfort. Nothing could so well have cheered the heart of Jesus, and taken his mind for just an instant off from his own bitter pangs, as having an object of pity before him upon whom he could pour his mercy. The thief's confession of faith and expiring prayer must have been music to his Saviour's ear, the only music which could in any degree delight him amid his terrible agonies. To hear and to answer the prayer, "Lord, remember me when thou comest into thy kingdom," afforded our Lord a precious solace. An angel strengthened him in the garden, but here it was a man, nailed up at his side, who ministered consolation by the indirect but very effective method of seeking help at his hands.

Furthermore, the long continued testimony and witness for Christ among men was at that time exceedingly feeble and ready to expire, and the thief's confession maintained it. The apostles, where were they? They had fled. Those disciples who ventured near enough to see the Lord scarcely remained within speaking distance. They were poor confessors of Christ, scarcely worthy of the name. Was the chain of testimony to be broken? Would none declare his sovereign power? No, the Lord will never let that testimony cease, and lo! he raises up a witness where least you would expect it—on the gibbet. One just ready to die bears witness to the Redeemer's innocence and to his assured coming to a kingdom. As many of the boldest testimonies to Christ have come from the stake, so here was one that came from the gibbet, and gained for the witness the honour of being the last testifier to Christ before he died.

Let us always expect, then, dear friends, that God will overrule the machinations of the foes of Christ so as to get honour

from them. At all times of the world's
history, when things appear to have gone
to pieces, and Satan seems to rule the
hour, do not let us despair, but be quite
sure that, somehow or other, light will
come out of darkness, and good out of evil.

We will now come close up to the dying
thief, and look, first, at *his faith*; secondly,
at *his confession of faith*; thirdly, at *his
prayer of faith*; and fourthly, at *the
answer to his faith.*

I. First, then, may the Holy Ghost
help us concerning this dying malefactor,
to consider HIS FAITH.

It was of the operation of the Spirit of
God, and there was *nothing in his previous
character to lead up to it*. How came that
thief to be a believer in Jesus? You
who carefully read the gospels will have
noticed that Matthew says (Matt. xxvii.
44) "the thieves also, which were crucified with him, cast the same in his teeth."
Mark also says, "They that were crucified
with him reviled him." These two evan-
gelists plainly speak of both thieves as
reviling our Lord. How are we to understand this? Would it be right to say
that those two writers speak in broad
terms of the thieves as a class, because

one of them so acted, just as we in common conversation speak of a company of persons doing so and so, when in fact the whole matter was the deed of one man of the party? Was it a loose way of speaking? I think not: I do not like the look of suppositions of error in the inspired volume. Would it not be more reverent to the word of God to believe that the thieves did both revile Jesus? May it not be true that, at the first, they both joined in saying, "If thou be the Christ save thyself and us," but that afterwards one, by a miracle of sovereign grace, was led to a change of mind, and became a believer? Or would this third theory meet the case, that at the first the thief who afterwards became a penitent, having no thought upon the matter, by his silence gave consent to his fellow's reviling so as fairly to come under the charge of being an accomplice therein: but when it gradually dawned upon his mind that he was under error as to this Jesus of Nazareth, it pleased God in infinite mercy to change his mind, so that he became a confessor of the truth, though he had at first silently assented to the blasphemy of his companion? It would

be idle to dogmatize, but we will gather
this lesson from it—that faith may enter
the mind, notwithstanding the sinful state
in which the man is found.  Grace can
transform a reviling thief into a penitent
believer.

*Neither do we know the outward means
which led to this man's conversion.*  We
can only suppose that he was affected by
seeing the Lord's patient demeanour, or,
perhaps, by hearing that prayer, " Father,
forgive them, for they know not what
they do."  Surely there was enough in
the sight of the crucified Lord with the
blessing of God's Spirit to turn a heart
of stone into flesh.  Possibly the inscrip-
tion over the head of our Lord may have
helped him—" Jesus of Nazareth, the
King of the Jews."  Being a Jew, he
knew something of the Scriptures, and
putting all the facts together, may he not
have seen in the prophecies a light which
gathered around the head of the sufferer,
and revealed him as the true Messiah?
Possibly the malefactor remembered
Isaiah's words, " He is despised and
rejected of men ; a man of sorrows, and
acquainted with grief : and we hid as it
were our faces from him ; he was despised,

and we esteemed him not." Or perhaps the saying of David, in the twenty-second Psalm, rushed upon his memory, "They pierced my hands and my feet." Other texts which he had learned in his youth at his mother's knee may have come before his mind, and putting all these together, he may have argued, "It may be. Perhaps it is. It is. It must be. I am sure it is. It is the Messiah, led as a lamb to the slaughter." All this is but our supposition, and it leads me to remark that there is much faith in this world which cometh, "not with observation," but is wrought in men by unknown instrumentalities, and so long as it really exists it matters very little how it entered the heart, for in every case it is the work of the Holy Ghost. The history of faith is of small importance compared with the quality of faith.

We do not know the origin of this man's faith, but we do know that *it was amazing faith under the circumstances*. I very gravely question whether there was ever greater faith in this world than the faith of this thief; for he, beyond all others, realized the painful and shameful death of the Lord Jesus, and yet believed.

We hear of our Lord's dying upon the cross, but we do not realize the circumstances ; and, indeed, even if we were to think upon that death very long and intently, we shall never realize the shame and weakness and misery which surrounded our Lord as that dying thief did, for he himself was suffering the pangs of crucifixion at the Saviour's side, and therefore to him it was no fiction, but a vivid reality.   Before him was the Christ in all his nakedness and ignominy surrounded by the mocking multitude, and dying in pain and weakness, and yet he believed him to be Lord and King.   What think you, sirs ?   Some of you say you find it hard to believe in Jesus, though you know that he is exalted in the highest heavens ; but had you seen him on the cross, had you seen his marred countenance and emaciated body, could you then have believed on him, and said, "Lord, remember me when thou comest into thy kingdom"?   Yes, you could have done so if the Spirit of God had created faith in you like to that of the thief ; but it would have been faith of the first order, a jewel of priceless value. As I said before, so say I again, the vivid sympathy of the thief with the shame and suffering of the Lord rendered his faith remarkable in the highest degree.

*This man's faith, moreover, was singularly clear and decided.* He rolled his whole salvation upon the Lord Jesus and said, "Lord, remember me when thou comest into thy kingdom." He did not offer a single plea fetched from his doings, his present feelings, or his sufferings; but he cast himself upon the generous heart of Christ. "Thou hast a kingdom : thou are coming to it. Lord, remember me when thou comest into it." That was all. I wish that some who have been professors for years had as clear a faith as the thief; but they are too often confused between law and gospel, works and grace, while this poor felon trusted in nothing but the Saviour and his mercy. Blessed be God for clear faith. I do rejoice to see it in such a case as this, so suddenly wrought and yet so perfect—so outspoken, so intelligent, so thoroughly restful.

That word "restful" reminds me of a lovely characteristic of his faith, namely, *its deep peace-giving power.* There is a world of rest in Jesus, in the thief's prayer, " Lord, remember me when thou comest into thy kingdom." A thought from Christ is all he wanted, and after the Lord said, "To-day shalt thou be with me in paradise," we never read that the petitioner said another word. I did think that perhaps he would have said, "Blessed be the name of the Lord for that sweet assurance. Now I can die in peace;" but his gratitude was too deep for words, and his peace so perfect that calm silence seemed most in harmony with it. Silence is the thaw of the soul, though it be the frost of the mouth; and when the soul flows most freely it feels the inadequacy of the narrow channel of the lips for its great waterfloods.

"Come, then, expressive silence, muse his praise."

He asked no alleviation of pain, but in perfect satisfaction died as calmly as saints do in their beds.

This is the kind of faith which we must all have if we would be saved. Whether we know how we come by it or not, it must be a faith which rolls itself upon Christ and a faith which consequently brings peace to the soul. Do you possess such faith, dear friend? If you do not, remember that you may die on a sudden, and then into Paradise you will never enter. Look well to this, and believe in the Lord Jesus at once.

II. Secondly, we are going to look at this man's CONFESSION OF FAITH. He had faith, and he confessed it. He could neither be baptized nor sit at the communion table, nor unite with the church below; he could not do any of those things which are most right and proper on the part of other Christians, but he did the best he could under the circumstances to confess his Lord.

He confessed Christ, first of all, almost of necessity, because *a holy indignation made him speak out.* He listened for a while to his brother thief, but while he was musing, the fire burned, then spake he with his tongue, for he could no longer bear to hear the innocent sufferer reviled. He said, "Dost not thou fear God, seeing thou art in the same condemnation? And we indeed justly; for we receive the due reward of our deeds : but this man hath done nothing amiss." Did this poor thief speak out so bravely, and can some of you silent Christians go up and down the streets, and hear men curse and blaspheme the name of Christ, and not feel stirred in spirit to defend his cause? While men are so loud in their revilings can you be quiet? The stones you tread on may well cry out against you. If all were Christians, and the world teemed with Jesus' praise, we might, perhaps, afford to be silent; but, amidst abounding superstition and loud-mouthed infidelity, we are bound to show our colours, and avow ourselves on Christ's side. We doubt not that the penitent thief would have owned his Lord apart from the railing of his comrade; but, as it happened, that reviling was the provoking cause. Does no such cause arouse *you?* Can you play the coward at such a time as this?

Observe next, that *he made a confession to an unsympathetic ear*. The other thief does not seem to have made any kind of reply to him, but it is feared that he died in sullen unbelief. The believing thief made his confession where he could not expect to gain approbation, yet he made it none the less clearly. How is it that some dear friends who love the Lord have never confessed their faith, even to their Christian brethren? You know how glad we should be to hear of what the Lord has

done for you, but yet we have not heard
it. There is a mother who would be so
happy if she did but know that her boy
was saved, or that her girl was converted,
and you have refused her that joy by your
silence. This poor thief spoke for Jesus
to one who did not enter into his religious
experience, and you have not even told
yours to those who would have communed
with you and rewarded you with comfort
and instruction. I cannot understand
cowardly lovers of Christ. How you
manage to smother your love so long I
cannot tell. Love is usually like a cough,
which speaks for itself, or a candle which
must be seen, or a sweet perfume which
is its own revealer : how it is that you
have been able to conceal the day which
has dawned in your hearts ? What can
be your motive for coming to Jesus by
night only ? I cannot understand your
riddle, and I hope you will explain it
away. Do confess Jesus if you love him,
for he bids you do it, and says, " He that
confesseth me before men, him will I confess before my Father which is in heaven."

Observe well that this poor thief's confession of faith *was attended with a confession of sin.* Though he was dying a

most horrible death by crucifixion, yet
he confessed that he was suffering justly.
"We indeed justly." He made his confession not only to God but to men, justify-
ing the law of his country under which he
was then suffering. True faith confesses
Christ, and, at the same time, confesses
its sin. There must be repentance of sin
and acknowledgment of it before God if
faith is to give proof of its truth. A
faith that never had a tear in its eye, or
a blush on its cheek, is not the faith of
God's elect. He who never felt the burden
of sin, never felt the sweetness of being
delivered from it. This poor thief is as
clear in the avowal of his own guilt as in
his witness to the Redeemer's innocence.
Reader, could we say the same of you?

The thief's confession of faith *was exceedingly honouring to the Lord Jesus
Christ*. He confessed that Jesus of
Nazareth had done nothing amiss, when
the crowd around the cross were condemning him with speech and gesture.
He honoured Christ by calling him Lord
while others mocked him; by believing in
his kingdom while he was dying on a cross,
and by entreating him to remember him
though he was in the agonies of death.

Do you say that this was not much? Well, I will make bold to ask many a professor whether he could honestly say that throughout the whole of his life he has done as much to honour Christ as this poor thief did in those few minutes. Some of you certainly have not, for you have never confessed him at all; and others have confessed him in such a formal manner that there was nothing in it. Oh, there have been times when, had you played the man, and said right straight out, in the midst of a ribald crew, "I do believe in him whom you scoff, and I know the sweetness of that dear name, which you trample under foot," you might have been the means of saving many souls; but you were silent, and whispered to yourself that prudence was the better part of valour, and so you allowed the honour of your Master to be trailed in the mire. Oh, had you, my sister, taken your stand in the family—had you said, "You may do what you will, but as for me, I will serve the Lord"—you might have honoured God far more than you have done; for I fear you have been living in a halting, hesitating style, giving way to a great deal which you knew was wrong, not bearing

your protest, not rebuking your brother in
his inquity, but studying your own peace
and comfort instead of seeking the Redeemer's glory.   We have heard people
talk about this dying thief as if he never
did anything for his Master ; but let me
ask the Christian church if it has not
members in its midst—gray-haired members, too, who have never, through fifty
years of profession, borne one such bravely
honest and explicit testimony for Christ
as this man did while he was agonizing on
the cross.   Remember, the man's hands
and feet were tortured, and he himself was
suffering from that natural fever which
attends upon crucifixion ; his spirit must
have melted within him with his dying
griefs, and yet he was as bold in rebuke,
as composed in prayer, and as calm in
spirit as if he was suffering nothing, and
thus he reflected much glory upon his
Lord.

One other point about this man's confession is worthy of notice, namely, that
*he was evidently anxious to change the mind
of his companion.*  He rebuked him, and
he reasoned with him.   Dear friends, I
must again put a personal question.   Are
there not many professing Christians who

have never manifested a tithe as much anxiety for the souls of others as this thief felt? You have been a church member ten years, but did you ever say as much to your brother as this dying thief said to the one who was hanging near him? Well, you have meant to do so. Yes, but did you ever do it? You reply that you have been very glad to join others in a meeting. I know that too, and so far, so good; but did you ever personally say as much to another as this dying man did to his old companion? I fear that some of you cannot say so. I, for my part, bless and magnify the grace of God which gave this man one of the sweet fruits of the Spirit, namely, holy charity towards the soul of another, so soon after he himself had come to believe in Jesus. May we all of us have it yet more and more!

III. So much for the confession of his faith: now a little, in the third place, about HIS PRAYER OF FAITH. "Lord, remember me when thou comest into thy kingdom."

*He addressed the dying Saviour as divine.* Wonderful faith this, to call him Lord who was " a worm and no man," and was hanging there upon the cross to die.

What shall we say of those who, now that he is exalted in the highest heavens, yet refuse to own his deity? This man had a clearer knowledge of Christ than they have. The Lord take the scales from their eyes, and make them to pray to Jesus as divine.

*He prayed to him also as having a kingdom.* That needed faith, did it not? He saw a dying man in the hands of his foes nailed to a cross, and yet he believed that he would come into a kingdom. He knew that Jesus would die before long, the marks of the death-agony were upon him, and yet he believed that he would come to a kingdom. O glorious faith! Dear friend, dost thou believe in Christ's kingdom? Dost thou believe that he reigns in heaven, and that he will come a second time to rule over all the earth? Dost thou believe in Christ as King of kings and Lord of lords? Then pray to him as such, "Lord, remember me when thou comest into thy kingdom." May God give you the faith which set this thief a-praying in so excellent a fashion.

Observe that *his prayer was for a spiritual blessing only.* The other thief said, "Save thyself and us": he meant,

"Save us from this cross. Deliver us from the death which now threatens us." He sought temporal benefits, but this man asked only to be remembered by Christ in his kingdom. Do your prayers run that way, dear friends? Then I bless the Lord that he has taught you to seek eternal rather than temporal blessings. If a sick man cares more for pardon than for health it is a good sign. Soul mercies will be prized above all others where faith is in active exercise.

*Observe how humbly he prays.* He did not ask for a place at Christ's right hand; he did not, in fact, ask the Lord to do anything for him, but only to "remember" him. Yet that "remember" is a great word, and he meant much by it. "Do give a thought to thy poor companion who now confesses his faith in thee. Do in thy glory dart one recollection of thy love upon poor me, and think on me for good." It was a very humble prayer, and all the sweeter for its lowliness. It showed his great faith in Jesus, for he believed that even to be remembered by him would be enough. "Give me but the crumbs that fall from thy table, and they shall suffice me: but a thought, Lord Jesus, but oné thought from thy loving mind, and that shall satisfy my soul."

Did not his prayer drip with faith as a honeycomb with honey? It seems to me as if laid asoak in his faith till it was saturated through and through with it, for *he prays so powerfully*, albeit so humbly. Consider what his character had been, and yet he says "Lord, remember *me* when thou comest into thy kingdom." Note well that it is a thief—an outcast, a criminal on the gallows-tree who thus prays. He is an outcast by his country's laws, and yet he turns to the King of heaven and asks to be remembered. Bad as he is he believes that the Lord Jesus will have mercy upon him. Oh, brave faith!

We see how strong that faith was, because he had no invitation so to pray. I do not know that he had ever heard Christ preach. No apostle had said to him, "Come to Christ, and you will find mercy," and yet he came to Jesus. Here comes an uninvited guest in the sweet bravery of holy confidence in Christ's majestic love; he comes boldly and pleads, "Lord, remember me." It was strong faith which thus pleaded. Remember, too, that he was upon the verge of death. He knew that he could not live very long, and probably expected the Roman bone-breaker to give him very soon the final blow; but in the very hour and article of death he cried, "Lord, remember me," with the strong confidence of a mighty faith. Glory be to God who wrought such a faith in such a man as this.

IV. We have done when we have mentioned, in the fourth place, THE ANSWER TO HIS FAITH.

We will only say that *his faith brought him to paradise.* We had a paradise once, and the first Adam lost it. Paradise has been regained by the second Adam, and he has prepared for believers an Eden above fairer than that first garden of delights below. Faith led the dying thief *to be with Christ* in paradise, which was best of all. "To-day shalt thou be *with me* in paradise." Whatever the joy of Christ, and the glory of Christ, the thief was there to see it and to share it as soon as Christ himself.

And it brought him paradise *that very day.* Sometimes a crucified man will be two or three days a-dying; Jesus, therefore, assures him that he shall not have long to suffer, and confirms it with a "verily," which was our Lord's strong word of asseveration,—"Verily I say unto thee, to-day shalt thou be with me in paradise." Such a portion will faith win for each of us, not to-day it may be, but one day. If we believe in Jesus Christ, who died for our sins, we shall be with him in the delights and happiness of the spirit-world, and with him in the paradise of everlasting glory. If we commenced to believe at once, and were to die immediately, we should be with Christ at once, as surely as if we had been converted fifty years ago. You cannot tell how short your life will be, but it is well to be ready. A friend was here last Sabbath-day of whom I heard this morning that he was ill, and in another hour that he was dead. It was short work; he was smitten down, and gone at once. That may be the lot of any one of you; and if it should be, you will have no cause whatever to fear it if you now like the thief trust yourself wholly in Jesus' hands, crying, "Lord, remember me when thou comest into thy kingdom."

The lesson of our text is not merely that Christ can save in our last extremity,

though that is true, but that now at this
moment Jesus is able to save us, and that if
saved at all, salvation must be an immediate and complete act, so that, come life
or come death, we are perfectly saved.
It will not take the Lord long to raise the
dead—in a moment, in the twinkling of
an eye, the dead shall be raised incor-
ruptible; and the Lord takes no time in
regenerating a soul. Dead souls live in
an instant when the breath of the Spirit
quickens them. Faith brings instantaneous
pardon. There is no course of probation
to go through, there are no attainments
to be sought after, and no protracted
efforts to be made in order to be saved.
Thou art saved if thou believest in Jesus.
The finished work of Christ is thine.
Thou art God's beloved, accepted, forgiven, adopted child. Saved thou art,
and saved thou shalt be for ever and ever
if thou believest.

Instantaneous salvation! Immediate
salvation! This the Spirit of God gives to
those who trust in Jesus. Thou needest
not wait till to-morrow's sun has dawned.
Talk not of a more convenient season.
Sitting where thou art, the almighty grace
of God can come upon thee and save thee,

and this shall be a sign unto thee that
Christ is born in thy heart the hope of
glory,—when thou believest in him as thy
pardon, righteousness, and all in all, thou
shalt have peace.  If thou dost but trust
thyself in Jesus' hands thou art a saved
soul, and the angels in heaven are singing
high praises to God and the Lamb on
thine account.  Farewell.

# SAUL OF TARSUS;

## OR,

# THE PATTERN CONVERT

"Howbeit for this cause I obtained mercy, that in me first Jesus Christ might shew forth all longsuffering, for a pattern to them which should hereafter believe on him to life everlasting."—1 Timothy i. 16.

IT is a vulgar error that the conversion of the apostle Paul was an uncommon and exceptional event, and that we cannot expect men to be saved now-a-days after the same fashion. It is said that the incident was an exception to all rules, a wonder altogether by itself. Now, my text is a flat contradiction to that notion, for it assures us that instead of the apostle as a receiver of the longsuffering and mercy of God being at all an exception to the rule, he was a model convert, and is to be regarded as a type and pattern of God's grace in other believers. The apostle's language in the text, " for a pattern," may mean that he was what printers call a first proof, an early impression from the engraving, a specimen of those to follow. He was the typical instance of divine longsuffering, the model after which others are fashioned. To use a metaphor from the artists' studio, Paul was the ideal sketch of a convert, an outline of the work of Jesus on mankind, a cartoon of divine longsuffering. Just as artists make sketches in charcoal as the basis of their work, which outlines they paint out as the picture proceeds, so did the Lord in the apostle's case make as it were a cartoon or outline sketch of his usual work of grace. That outline in the case of each future believer he works out with infinite variety of skill, and produces the individual Christian, but the guiding lines are really there. All conversions are in a high degree similar to this pattern conversion. The transformation of persecuting Saul of Tarsus into the apostle Paul is a typical instance of the work of grace in the heart.

We will have no other preface, but proceed at once to two or three considerations.

The first is that IN THE CONVERSION OF
PAUL THE LORD HAD AN EYE TO OTHERS,
AND IN THIS PAUL IS A PATTERN. In
every case the individual is saved not for
himself alone, but with a view to the good
of others. Those who think the doctrine
of election to be harsh should not deny it,
for it is Scriptural ; but they may to their
own minds soften some of its hardness by
remembering that elect men bear a marked
connection with the race. The Jews as an
elect people were chosen in order to preserve the oracles of God for all nations
and for all times. Men personally elected
unto eternal life by divine grace are also
elected that they may become chosen
vessels to bear the name of Jesus unto
others. While our Lord is said to be the
Saviour specially of them that believe, he
is also called the Saviour of all men ; and
while he has a special eye to the good of
the one person whom he has chosen, yet
through that person he has designs of
love to others, perhaps even to thousands
yet unborn.

The apostle Paul says, " I obtained
mercy, that in me foremost Jesus Christ
might shew forth all longsuffering, for a
pattern to them which should hereafter

believe." Now, I think I see very clearly
that *Paul's conversion had an immediate
relation to the conversion of many others.*
It had a tendency, had it not, to excite an
interest in the minds of his brother
Pharisees? Men of his class, men of cul-
ture, who were equally at home with the
Greek philosophers and with the Jewish
rabbis, men of influence, men of rank,
would be sure to enquire, "What is this
new religion which has fascinated Saul of
Tarsus? That zealot for Judaism has now
become a zealot for Christianity: what can
there be in it?" I say that the natural
tendency of his conversion was to awaken
enquiry and thought, and so to lead others
of his rank to become believers. And, my
dear friend, if you have been saved, you
ought to regard it as a token of God's mercy
to your class. If you are a working man, let
your salvation be a blessing to the men with
whom you labour. If you are a person of
rank and station, consider that God intends to bless you to some with whom you
are on familiar terms. If you are young,
hope that God will bless the youth around
you, and if you have come to older years,
hope that your conversion, even at the
eleventh hour, may be the means of en-

couraging other aged pilgrims to seek and find rest unto their souls. The Lord, by calling one out of any society of men, finds for himself a recruiting officer who will enlist his fellows beneath the banner of the cross. May not this fact encourage some seeking soul to hope that the Lord may save him, though he be the only thoughtful person in all his family, and then make him to be the means of salvation to all his kindred.

We notice that *Paul often used the narrative of his conversion as an encouragement to others.* He was not ashamed to tell his own life-story. Eminent soul-winners such as Whitefield and Bunyan frequently pleaded God's mercy to themselves as an argument with their fellowmen. Though great preachers of another school, such as Robert Hall and Chalmers, do not mention themselves at all, and I can admire their abstinence, yet I am persuaded that if some of us were to follow their example we should be throwing away one of the most powerful weapons of our warfare. What can be more affecting, more convincing, more overwhelming than the story of divine grace told by the very man who has experienced it? It is

better than a score tales of converted
Africans, and infinitely more likely to win
men's hearts than the most elaborate
essays upon moral excellence.  Again and
again Paul gave a long narrative of his
conversion, for he felt it to be one of the
most telling things that he could relate.
Whether he stood before Felix or Agrippa,
this was his plea for the gospel.  All
through his epistles there are continual
mentions of the grace of God towards himself, and we may be sure that the apostle
did right thus to argue from his own case :
it is fair and forcible reasoning and ought
by no means to be left unused because
of a selfish dread of being called egotis-
tical.  God intends that we should use our
conversion as an encouragement to others,
and say to them, " Come and hear, all ye
that fear God, and I will tell you what he
has done for my soul."  We point to our
own forgiveness and say, " Do but trust
in the living Redeemer, and you shall find,
as we have done, that Jesus blotteth out
the transgressions of believers."

*Paul's conversion was an encourage-
ment to him all his life long to have hope
for others.*  Have you ever read the first
chapter of the Epistle to the Romans ?

Well, the man who penned those terrible verses might very naturally have written at the end of them—"Can these monsters be reclaimed? It can be of no avail whatever to preach the gospel to people so sunken in vice." That one chapter gives as daring an outline as delicacy would permit of the nameless, shameful vices into which the heathen world had plunged, and yet, after all, Paul went forth to declare the gospel to that filthy and corrupt generation, believing that God meant to save a people out of it. Surely one element of his hope for humanity must have been found in the fact of his own salvation; he considered himself to be in some respects as bad as the heathen, and in other respects even worse: he calls himself the *foremost* of sinners (that is the word); and he speaks of God having saved him foremost, that in him he might show forth all longsuffering. Paul never doubted the possibility of the conversion of a person however infamous after he had been converted himself. This strengthened him in battling with the fiercest opponents—he who overcame such a wild beast as I was, can also tame others and bring them into willing captivity to his love.

There was yet another relation between Paul's conversion and the salvation of others, and it was this:—*It served as an impulse,* driving him forward in his life-work of bringing sinners to Christ. " I obtained mercy," said he, " and that same voice which spake peace to me said, I have made thee a chosen vessel unto me to bear my name among the Gentiles." And he did bear it, my brethren. Going into regions beyond that, he might not build on another man's foundation, he became a master builder for the Church of God. How indefatigably did he labour! With what vehemence did he pray! With what energy did he preach! Slander and contempt he bore with the utmost patience. Scourging or stoning had no terrors for him. Imprisonment, yea death itself, he defied; nothing could daunt him. Because the Lord had saved him he felt that he must by all means save some. He could not be quiet. Divine love was in him like a fire, and if he had been silent he would ere long have had to cry with the prophet of old, " I am weary with restraining." He is the man who said, " Necessity is laid upon me, yea woe is unto me if I preach not the gospel." Paul, the extraordinary sinner, was saved that he might be full of extraordinary zeal and bring multitudes to eternal life. Well could he say,

> " The love of Christ doth me constrain
> To seek the wandering souls of men ;
> With cries, entreaties, tears to save,
> To snatch them from the fiery wave.
>
> My life, my blood I here present,
> If for Thy truth they may be spent ;
> Fulfil Thy sovereign counsel, Lord !
> Thy will be done, Thy name adored !"

Now, I will pause here a minute to put a question. You profess to be converted, my dear friend. What relation has your conversion already had to other people ? It ought to have a very apparent one. Has it had such ? Mr. Whitefield said that when his heart was renewed his first desire was that his companions with whom he had previously wasted his time might be brought to Christ. It was natural and commendable that he should begin with them. Remember how one of the apostles, when he discovered the Saviour, went immediately to tell his brother. It is most fitting that young people should spend their first religious enthusiasm upon their brothers and sisters. As to converted parents, their first responsibility is in reference to their sons and daughters. Upon each renewed man his natural affinities, or the bonds of friendship, or the looser ties of neighbourhood should begin to operate at once, and each one should feel—"No man liveth unto himself." If divine grace has kindled a fire in you it is that your fellow men may burn with the same flame. If the eternal fount has filled you with living water it is that out of the midst of you should flow rivers of living water. You are blessed that you may bless; whom have you blessed yet? Let the question go round. Do not avoid it. This is the best return that you can make to God, that when he saveth you you should seek to be the instruments in his hands of saving others. What have you done yet? Did you ever speak with the friend who shares your pew? He has been sitting there for a long time, and may perhaps be an unconverted person; have you pointed him to the Lamb of God? Have you ever spoken to your servants about their souls? Have you yet broken the ice sufficiently to speak to your own sister, or your own brother?

Do begin, dear friend.   That Christianity
which is consistent with selfishness is not
consistent with Christ.   You do not possess the spirit of Christ if the only thing
you seek for is your own salvation ; and if
any man have not the Spirit of Christ he
is none of his.

Are you ashamed of your negligence in
the past, then bestir yourself for the
future.   Vain regrets cannot redeem lost
opportunities, but holy resolves may prevent future omissions.   Come now, what
can you do ?   What will you do ?   Take
counsel with a grateful heart and be no
longer a dumb dog, a fruitless tree, a blot
and a blank in the church of God.

You cannot tell what mysterious threads
connect you with your fellow men and
their destiny.   There was a cobbler once,
as you know, in Northamptonshire.   Who
could see any connection between him
and the millions of India ?   But the love
of God was in his bosom, and Carey could
not rest till at Serampore he had commenced to translate the Word of God and
preach to his fellow men.   We must not
confine our thoughts to the few whom
Carey brought to Christ, though to save
one soul is worthy of a life of sacrifice,

but Carey became the forerunner and leader of a missionary band which will never cease to labour till India bows before Immanuel. That man mysteriously drew, is drawing, and will draw India to the Lord Jesus Christ. Brother, you do not know what your power is. Awake and try it. Did you never read this passage: "Thou hast given him power over all flesh, that he should give eternal life to as many as thou hast given him"? Now, the Lord has given to his Son power over all flesh, and with a part of that power Jesus clothes his servants. Through you he will give eternal life to certain of his chosen; by you and by no other means will they be brought to himself. Look about you, regenerate man. Your life may be made sublime. Rouse yourself! Begin to think of what God may do by you! Calculate the possibilities which lie before you with the eternal God as your helper. Shake yourself from the dust and put on the beautiful garments of disinterested love to others, and it shall yet be seen how grandly gracious God has been to hundreds of men by having converted you.

So far, then, Paul's salvation, because

it had so clear a reference to others, was a pattern of all conversions.

II. Now, secondly, PAUL'S FOREMOST POSITION AS A SINNER DID NOT PREVENT HIS BECOMING FOREMOST IN GRACE, AND HEREIN AGAIN HE IS A PATTERN TO US. Foremost in sin, he became also foremost in service. Saul of Tarsus was a *blasphemer*, and he is to be commended because he has not recorded any of those blasphemies. We can never object to converted burglars and chimney-sweepers, of whom we hear so much, telling the story of their conversion; but when they go into dirty details they had better hold their tongues. Paul tells us that he was a blasphemer, but he never repeats one of the blasphemies. We invent enough evil in our own hearts without being told of other men's stale profanities. If, however, any of you are so curious as to want to know what kind of blasphemies Paul could utter, you have only to converse with a converted Jew and he will tell you what horrible words some of his nation will speak against our Lord. I have no doubt that Paul in his evil state thought as wickedly of Christ as he could—considered him to be an impostor, called him

so, and added many an opprobrious epithet.
He does not say of himself that he was an
unbeliever and an objector, but he says
that he was a  blasphemer, which is a
very strong word, but not too strong, for
the apostle never went beyond the truth.
He was a downright, thorough-going
blasphemer, who also caused others to
blaspheme.    Will these lines meet the eye
of a profane person who feels the greatness of his sin ?    May God grant that he
may be encouraged to seek mercy as Saul
of Tarsus did, for " all manner of sin and
of blasphemy did he forgive unto men."

From blasphemy, which was the sin of
the lips, Saul proceeded to *persecution*,
which is a sin of the hands.    Hating
Christ, he hated his people too.    He was
delighted to give his vote for the death of
Stephen, and he took care of the clothes
of those who stoned that martyr.    He
haled men and women to prison, and compelled them to blaspheme.    When he had
hunted all Judea as closely as he could he
obtained letters to go to Damascus, that
he might do the same in that place.    His
prey had been compelled to quit Jerusalem
and fly to more remote places, but " being
exceeding mad against them he perse-

cuted them unto strange cities." He was foremost in blasphemy and persecution. Will a persecutor read or hear these words ? If so, may he be led to see that even for him pardon is possible. Jesus who said, " Father, forgive them ; for they know not what they do," is still an intercessor for the most violent of his enemies.

He adds, next, that he was *injurious*, which I think Bengel considers to mean that he was a despiser : that eminent critic says—blasphemy was his sin towards God, persecution was his sin towards the church, and despising was his sin in his own heart. He was injurious—that is, he did all he could to damage the cause of Christ, and he thereby injured himself. He kicked against the pricks and injured his own conscience. He was so determined against Christ that he counted no cost too great by which he might hinder the spread of the faith, and he did hinder it terribly. He was a ringleader in re-sisting the Spirit of God which was then working with the church of Christ. He was foremost in opposition to the cross of Christ.

Now, notice that he was saved as a pattern, which is to show you that if

you also have been foremost in sin you
also may obtain mercy as Paul did: and
to show you yet again that if you have not
been foremost, the grace of God, which
is able to save the chief of sinners, can assuredly save those who are of less degree.
If the bridge of grace will carry the ele-
phant it will certainly carry the mouse.
If the mercy of God could bear with the
hugest sinners it can have patience with
you. If a gate is wide enough for a giant
to pass through, any ordinary sized mortal
will find space enough. Despair's head is
cut off and stuck on a pole by the salvation of "the chief of sinners." No man
can now say that he is too great a sinner
to be saved, because the chief of sinners
was saved eighteen hundred years ago.
If the ringleader, the chief of the gang,
has been washed in the precious blood,
and is now in heaven, why not I? why
not *you?*

After Paul was saved he became a foremost saint. The Lord did not allot him
a second-class place in the church. He
had been the leading sinner, but his Lord
did not, therefore, say, "I save you, but
I shall always remember your wickedness
to your disadvantage." Not so: he counted

him faithful, putting him into the minis-
try and into the apostleship, so that he was
not a whit behind the very chief of the
apostles. Brother, there is no reason why,
if you have gone very far in sin, you
should not go equally far in usefulness.
On the contrary there is a reason why
you should do so, for it is a rule of grace
that to whom much is forgiven the same
loveth much, and much love leads to much
service. What man was more clear in
his knowledge of doctrine than Paul?
What man more earnest in the defence of
truth? What man more self-sacrificing?
What man more heroic? The name of
Paul in the Christian church stands in
some respects the very next to the Lord
Jesus. Turn to the New Testament and
see how large a space is occupied by the
Holy Spirit speaking through his servant
Paul; and then look over Christendom and
see how greatly the man's influence is still
felt, and must be felt till his Master shall
come. Oh, great sinner, if thou art even
now ready to scoff at Christ, my prayer is
that he may strike thee down at this very
moment, and turn thee into one of his
children, and make thee to be just as
ardent for the truth as thou art now

earnest against it, as desperately set on good as now thou art on evil. None make such mighty Christians and such fervent preachers as those who are lifted up from the lowest depths of sin and washed and purified through the blood of Jesus Christ. May grace do this with thee, my dear friend, whoever thou mayest be.

Thus we gather from our text that the Lord showed mercy to Paul that in him foremost it might be seen that prominence in sin is no barrier to eminence in grace, but the very reverse.

III. Now I come to where the stress of the text lies. PAUL'S CASE WAS A PATTERN OF OTHER CONVERSIONS AS AN INSTANCE OF LONGSUFFERING. "That in me foremost Jesus Christ might show forth all longsuffering for a cartoon or pattern to them which should hereafter believe." Thoughtfully observe the great longsuffering of God to Paul: he says, "He showed forth all longsuffering." Not only all the longsuffering of God that ever was shown to anybody else, but all that could be supposed to exist—*all* longsuffering.

> "All thy mercy's height I prove,
>   All its depth is found in me,"

as if he had gone to the utmost stretch of his tether in sin, and the Lord also had strained his longsuffering to its utmost.

That longsuffering was seen first in sparing his life when he was rushing headlong in sin, breathing out threatenings, foaming at the mouth with denunciations of the Nazarene and his people. If the Lord had but lifted his finger Saul would have been crushed like a moth, but almighty wrath forbore, and the rebel lived on. Nor was this all; after all his sin the Lord allowed mercy to be possible to him. He blasphemed, and persecuted at a red-hot rate; and is it not a marvel that the Lord did not say, "Now at last you have gone beyond all bearing, and you shall die like Herod, eaten of worms"? It would not have been at all wonderful if God had so sentenced him; but he allowed him to live within the reach of mercy, and, better still, he in due time actually sent the gospel to him, and laid it home to his heart. In the very midst of his rebellion the Lord saved him. He had not prayed to be converted, far from it; no doubt he had that very day along the road to Damascus, profaned the Saviour's name, and yet mighty mercy

burst in and saved him purely by its own
spontaneous native energy. Oh mighty
grace, free grace, victorious grace! This
was longsuffering indeed!

When divine mercy had called Paul
it swept all his sin away, every particle of
it, his blood shedding and his blasphemy,
all at once, so that never man was more
assured of his own perfect cleansing than
was the apostle. "There is therefore now,"
saith he, "no condemnation to them which
are in Christ Jesus." "Therefore being
justified by faith, we have peace with
God." "Who shall lay anything to the
charge of God's elect?" You know how
clear he was about that ; and he spoke out
of his own experience. Longsuffering had
washed all his sins away. Then that longsuffering reaching from the depths of sin
lifted him right up to the apostleship, so
that he began to prove God's longsuffering
in its heights of favour. What a privilege
it must have been to him to be permitted
to preach the gospel. I should think
sometimes when he was preaching most
earnestly he would half stop himself and
say, " Paul, is this you?" When he went
down to Tarsus especially he must have
been surprised at himself and at the

mighty mercy of God. He preached the faith which once he had destroyed. He must have said many a time after a sermon when he went home to his bedchamber, " Marvel of marvels ! Wonder of wonders that I who once could curse have now been made to preach—that I, who was full of threatening and even breathed out slaughter, should now be so inspired by the Spirit of God that I weep at the very sound of Jesus's name, and count all things but loss for the excellency of the knowledge of Christ Jesus my Lord." Oh, brothers and sisters, you do not measure long-suffering except you take it in all its length from one end to the other, and see God in mercy not remembering his servant's sin, but lifting him into eminent service in his church. Now, this was for a pattern, to show you that he will show forth the same longsuffering to those who believe. If you have been a swearer he will cleanse your blackened mouth, and put his praises into it. Have you had a black, cruel heart, full of enmity to Jesus ? He will remove it and give you a new heart and a right spirit. Have you dived into all sorts of sins ? Are they so shameful that you dare not think of them? Think of the precious blood which removes every stain. Are your sins so many that you could not count them? Do you feel as if you were almost damned already in the very memory of your life? I do not wonder at it, but he is able to save to the uttermost them that come unto God by him. You have not gone farther than Saul had gone, and therefore all longsuffering can come to you, and there are great possibilities of future holiness and usefulness before you. Even though you may have been a street-walker or a thief, yet if the grace of God cleanses you it can make something wonderful out of you: full many a lustrous jewel of Immanuel's crown has been taken from the dunghill. You are a rough block of stone, but Jesus can fashion and polish you and set you as a pillar in his temple. Brother, do not despair. See what Saul was and what Paul became, and learn what you may be. Though you deserve the depths of hell, yet up to the heights of heaven grace can lift you. Though now you feel as if the fiends of the pit would be fit companions for such a lost spirit as yourself, yet believe in the Lord Jesus and you shall one day walk among the angels as pure and white as they. Paul's experience of longsuffering grace was meant to be a pattern of what God will do for you.

" Scripture says, 'Where sin abounded,
  There did grace much more abound :'
Thus has Satan been confounded,
  And his own discomfit found.
    Christ has triumph'd !
Spread the glorious news around.

Sin is strong, but grace is stronger ;
  Christ than Satan more supreme ;
Yield, oh, yield to sin no longer,
  Turn to Jesus, yield to Him—
    He has triumph'd !
Sinners, henceforth Him esteem."

IV. Again, THE MODE OF PAUL'S CONVERSION WAS ALSO MEANT TO BE A PATTERN, and with this I shall finish. I do not say that we may expect to receive the miraculous revelation which was given to Paul, but yet it is a sketch upon which any conversion can be painted. The filling up is not the same in any two cases, but the outline sketch of Paul's conversion would serve for an outline sketch of the conversion of any one of us. How was that conversion wrought ? Well, it is clear that *there was nothing at all in Paul to*

*contribute to his salvation.* You might
have sifted him in a sieve, without
finding anything upon which you could
rest a hope that he would be converted
to the faith of Jesus. His natural bent,
his early training, his whole surroundings,
and his life's pursuits, all fettered him to
Judaism, and made it most unlikely that
he would ever become a Christian. The
first elder of the church that ever talked
to him about divine things could hardly
believe in his conversion. "Lord," said he,
"I have heard by many of this man, how
much evil he hath done to thy saints at
Jerusalem." He could hardly think it possible that the ravening wolf should have
changed into a lamb. Nothing favourable
to faith in Jesus could have been found
in Saul ; the soil of his heart was very
rocky, the ploughshare could not touch it,
and the good seed found no roothold. Yet
the Lord converted Saul, and he can do
the like by other sinners, but it must be
a work of pure grace and of divine power,
for there is not in any man's fallen nature
a holy spot of the size of a pin's point on
which grace can light. Transforming
grace can find no natural lodgment in
our hearts, it must create its own soil ;

and, blessed be God, it can do it, for with God all things are possible. Nature contributes nothing to grace, and yet grace wins the day. Humbled soul, let this cheer thee. Though there is nothing good in thee, yet grace can work wonders, and save thee by its own might.

Paul's conversion was an instance of divine power, and of that alone, and so is every true conversion. If your conversion is an instance of the preacher's power you need to be converted again; if your salvation is the result of your own power it is a miserable deception, from which may you be delivered. Every man who is saved must be operated upon by the might of God the Holy Spirit: every jot and tittle of true regeneration is the Spirit's work. As for our strength, it warreth against salvation rather than for it. Blessed is that promise, "Thy people shall be willing in the day of thy power." Conversion is as much a work of God's omnipotence as the resurrection; and as the dead do not raise themselves, so neither do men convert themselves.

*But Saul was changed immediately.* His conversion was once done and done at once. There was a little interval before he found peace, but even during those three days he was a changed man, though he was in sadness. He was under the power of Satan at one moment, and in the next he was under the reign of grace. This is also true in every conversion. However gradual the breaking of the day there is a time when the sun is below the horizon and a moment when he is no longer so. You may not know the exact time in which you passed from death to life, but there was such a time, if you are indeed a believer. A man may not know how old he is, but there was a moment in which he was born. In every conversion there is a distinct change from darkness to light, from death to life, just as certainly as there was in Paul's. And what a delightful hope does the rapidity of regeneration present to us! It is by no long and laborious process that we escape from sin. We are not compelled to remain in sin for a single moment. Grace brings instantaneous liberty to those who sit in bondage. He who trusts Jesus is saved on the spot. Why then abide in death? Why not lift up your eyes to immediate life and light?

*Paul proved his regeneration by his faith.* He believed unto eternal life. He tells us

over and over again in his epistles that he
was saved by faith, and not by works.
So is it with every man; if saved at all it
is by simply believing in the Lord Jesus.
Paul esteemed his own works to be less
than nothing, and called them dross and
dung, that he might win Christ, and so
every converted man renounces his own
works that he may be saved by grace
alone. Whether he has been moral or
immoral, whether he has lived an amiable
and excellent life or whether he has raked
in the kennels of sin, every regenerate
man has one only hope, and that is centred
and fixed in Jesus alone. Faith in Jesus
Christ is the mark of salvation, even as
the heaving of the lungs or the coming
of breath from the nostrils is the test
of life. Faith is the grace which saves
the soul, and its absence is a fatal
sign. How does this fact affect you, dear
friend? Hast thou faith or no?

*Paul was very positively and evidently
saved.* You did not need to ask the question, Is that man a Christian or not? for
the transformation was most apparent. If
Saul of Tarsus had appeared as he used to
be, and Paul the apostle could also have
come in, and you could have seen the one

man as two men, you would have thought
them no relation to one another.    Paul the
apostle would have said that he was dead
to Saul of Tarsus, and Saul of Tarsus
would have gnashed his teeth at Paul the
apostle.   The change was evident to all
who knew him, whether they sympathize
in it or not.   They could not mistake the
remarkable   difference   which   grace had
made, for it was as great as when midnight brightens into noon.   So it is when
a man is truly saved : there is a change
which those around him must perceive.
Do not tell me that you can be a child
at home and become a Christian and yet
your father and mother will not perceive
a difference in you.   They will be sure
to see it.   Would a leopard in a menagerie
lose his spots and no one notice it ?
Would an Ethiopian be turned white and
no one hear of it ?   You, masters and mistresses, will not go in and out amongst
your servants and children without their
perceiving a change in you if you are
born again.   At least, dear brother or
sister, strive with all your might to let the
change be very apparent in your language,
in your actions, and in your whole conduct.   Let your conversation be such as

becometh the gospel of Christ, that men may see that you as well as the apostle are decidedly changed by the renewal of your minds.

May all of us be the subjects of divine grace as Paul was : stopped in our mad career, blinded by the glory of the heavenly light, called by a mysterious voice, conscious of natural blindness, relieved of blinding scales, and made to see Jesus as one all in all. May we prove in our own persons how speedily conviction may melt into conversion, conversion into confession, and confession into consecration.

I have done when I have enquired, how far we are conformed to the pattern which God has set before us ? I know we are like Paul as to our sin, for if we have neither blasphemed nor persecuted, yet have we sinned as far as we have had opportunity. We are also conformed to Paul's pattern in the great longsuffering of God which we have experienced, and I am not sure that we cannot carry the parallel farther : we have had much the same revelation that Paul received on the way to Damascus, for we too have learned that Jesus is the Christ. If any of us sin against

Christ it will not be because we do not know him to be the Son of God, for we all believe in his Deity, because our Bibles tell us so. The pattern goes so far: I would that the grace of God would operate upon you, unconverted friend, and complete the picture, by giving you like faith with Paul. Then will you be saved as Paul was. Then also you will love Christ above all things as Paul did, and you will say: "But what things were gain to me, those I counted loss for Christ. Yea doubtless, and I count all things but loss for the excellency of the knowledge of Christ Jesus my Lord." He rested upon what Christ had done in his death and resurrection, and he found pardon and eternal life at once, and became, therefore, a devoted Christian.

What sayest thou, dear friend? Art thou moved to follow Paul's example? Does the Spirit of God prompt thee to trust Paul's Saviour, and give up every other ground of trust and rely upon him? Then do so and live. Does there seem to be a hand holding thee back, and dost thou hear an evil whisper saying, "Thou art too great a sinner"? Turn round and bid the fiend depart, for the text gives him the lie. "In me *foremost* hath Jesus Christ showed forth all long-suffering for a pattern to them which should hereafter believe on his name." God has saved Paul. Back, then, O devil! The Lord can save any man, and he can save me. Jesus Christ of Nazareth is mighty to save, and I will rely on him. If any poor heart shall reason thus its logic will be sound and unanswerable. Mercy to one is an argument for mercy to another, for there is no difference, but the same Lord over all is rich unto all that call upon him.

Now I have set the case before you, and I cannot do more; it remains with each individual to accept or refuse. One man can bring a horse to the trough, but a hundred cannot make him drink. There is the gospel; if you want it take it, but if you will not have it then I must discharge my soul by reminding you that even the gentle gospel—the gospel of love and mercy has nothing to say to you but this—"He that believeth not shall be damned." It is not the law which speaks thus sternly, but the gospel. It shakes the dust from off its feet against you if you reject its loving invitations.

If you count yourselves unworthy of infinite mercy, that very forgiveness which you now may have for nothing, will if rejected become the surest evidence of your black-hearted enmity against the Lord.

> "How they deserve the deepest hell
>     That slight the joys above ;
> What chains of vengeance must they feel
>     Who break the bonds of love."

God grant that you may yield to mighty love, and find peace in Christ Jesus.

# THE PHILIPPIAN JAILOR;

## OR,

# THE GOOD OFFICER IMPROVED

" Who, having received such a charge, thrust them into
the inner prison, and made their feet fast in the stocks.
And at midnight Paul and Silas prayed, and sang praises
unto God : and the prisoners heard them.  And suddenly
there was a great earthquake, so that the foundations of
the prison were shaken : and immediately all the doors
were opened, and every one's bands were loosed.  And the
keeper of the prison awaking out of his sleep, and seeing
the prison doors open, he drew out his sword, and would
have killed himself, supposing that the prisoners had been
fled.  But Paul cried with a loud voice, saying, Do thyself
no harm : for we are all here.  Then he called for a light,
and sprang in, and came trembling, and fell down before
Paul and Silas.  And brought them out, and said, Sirs,
what must I do to be saved?  And they said, Believe on
the Lord Jesus Christ, and thou shalt be saved, and thy
house.  And they spake unto him the word of the Lord,
and to all that were in his house.  And he took them the
same hour of the night, and washed their stripes ; and was
baptized, he and all his, straightway.  And when he had
brought them into his house, he set meat before them,
and rejoiced, believing in God with all his house."—
Acts xvi. 24--34.

THE work of God at Philippi went on
very quietly and successfully in the hands

of Paul and Silas. It was the commence-
ment of the gospel in Europe, and very
auspicious were its circumstances. The
good work was intimately connected with
prayer-meetings, which for this reason
should always wear a charm for Europeans.

Godly women met together for devotion,
Paul spoke to them, and households were
converted and baptized. The work went
on delightfully, but the devil, as usual,
must needs put his foot in. To any who
judged according to the sight of the eyes
it must have seemed a most unfortunate
circumstance that a poor woman having a
spirit of divination came in Paul's way. It
was a sad ruffling of the gentle stream
of prosperity when, on account of his cast-
ing the demon out of her, the apostle and
his companion were dragged by the mob
before the magistrates, shamefully beaten,
and thrown into prison. Now the
preacher's mouth would be stopped, so far
as the people of Philippi outside the jail
gates were concerned. No more of those
delightful prayer-meetings and Bible read-
ings, and openings up of the Scriptures.
Surely there was cause for the deepest
regret. It might have appeared so, but
like a great many other incidents con-

nected with Christian work, the matter
could not be judged by the outward ap-
pearance, for the Lord had a secret and
blessed design, which was being answered
by the apparent disaster.    Servants of
Jesus Christ, never be discouraged when
you are opposed, but when things run
counter to your wishes expect that the Lord
has provided some better thing for you.
He is driving you away from shallow
waters and bringing you into deeper seas,
where your nets shall bring you larger
draughts.  Paul and Silas must go to
prison because a chosen person was to be
converted in the prison, who could not
otherwise be reached.

Nay, it was not one person only who was
to be saved, but eternal love had fixed its
eye upon a whole house.  The members of
this elect family could by no other means
be brought to Christ but through Paul
and Silas being cast into prison ; and,
therefore, into prison they must go, to do
more by night in their bonds than they
could have done by day if they had
been free, and to bring to Christ some that
would be more illustrious trophies of the
grace of God than any they could have
gathered had they been preaching in the

streets of Philippi. God knows where it is best for his servants to be, and how it is best for them to be. If he foresees that they will do more good with their backs scarred than they would have done if they had escaped the flagellation, then their bodies must bear the marks of the Lord Jesus, and they must rejoice to have it so. Brethren, we do not like the sick bed; we would not choose aching limbs, especially those of us who are of an active disposition, and would fain be perpetually telling out the love of Christ; and yet in our temporary imprisonment we have seen the Lord's wisdom, and have had to look back with thankfulness upon it. Oh, children of God, your Father knows best. Leave everything in his hands, and be at peace, for all is well. May the Holy Ghost work quietness of heart in you.

Our subject is the jailor of Philippi: and, first, we shall say a little as to *what kind of man he was before conversion;* secondly, we shall consider *what was the occasion of his conversion;* and then, thirdly, we will notice *what sort of convert he made* when the grace of God brought him to Jesus' feet.

**I.** First, then, WHAT SORT OF MAN WAS THIS JAILOR? The jailor is a remarkable instance of the power of divine grace, but he ought not to be spoken of as a notably great transgressor, for of this there is no trace whatever. He was, like ourselves, full of sin and iniquity, but we find no record of anything specially bad about him. I see no reason why Mr. Wesley should so severely stigmatize him as he does in his lines:

" What but the power which wakes the dead
  Could reach a stubborn gaoler's heart,
  In cruelty and rapine bred,
  Who took the ancient murderer's part?
  Could make a harden'd ruffian feel,
  And shake him o'er the mouth of hell?"

On the contrary, we shall be able to show that the jailor's salvation is an instance of the grace of God saving one of an admirable moral character, one in whom there were most commendable points, a man of such regularity and decision, that he was not so much saved from vice as from self-righteousness. I take it, from the little we know of him, that he was a fine specimen of stern Roman discipline, *a man full of respect for those in authority, and prompt in obedience to orders.* He was a jailor, and he had to act, not on his own responsibility, but on the command of others, and he scrupulously did so. When we read, "having received *such a charge*," we infer that he carefully followed the tenor of his orders, and attentively observed the weight which the magistrates threw into them. He therefore thrust the apostle and his friend into the inner prison and made their feet fast in the stocks. You can see that he was thorough-going in obedience to authority; for afterwards, although he might have liked to retain the apostle and Silas in his house, yet, when the magistrates sent him word, he spoke to his beloved guests as an official was bound to do, waiving, in some respects, the friend, and tersely saying, "The magistrates have sent to let you go; now, therefore depart, and go in peace." It strikes me that he was an old soldier—a legionary who had fought and done rough work in his younger days, and then settled down, appointed on account of his good behaviour to the important post of governor of the jail of Philippi. With his family about him, he occupied himself in attending to his duties as a jailor, and carried them out with the strictest regularity. For this he is to be commended; for, it is expected of men that they be found faithful.

I say, then, that I regard him as an instance of a man whose mind was moulded according to the Roman type, a person subservient to discipline, and strict in obedience to rule. I grant that there was a little harshness about his fulfilling the orders concerning Paul and Silas, for he seems to have "*thrust*" them into the dungeon with some violence; but we cannot object to their being placed in the inner prison, or to their feet being made fast in the stocks, because his orders were that he should keep them safely, and he was only doing his best to do so. He was not responsible for the order of the magistrates; and when the prisoners were brought to him fresh from the lictor's rods with a strict charge, what was he to do but to obey it to the letter? He did so, and does not deserve to be called a ruffian for it. His ruling idea was that he was a servant of the government and bound to carry out his instructions, and was he not right? Such men are very

needful in government employ, and I
cannot tell how public business could be
done without them.

Notice that before he went to bed he
saw that the prison doors were all fastened,
and the lights put out. Even Roman
jailors were open to bribes, and though
lights had to be extinguished at a certain
hour of the night, it was possible to burn
your lamp still, if you placed a little oil
upon the jailor's palm. But there was no
lamp in the jail of Philippi, for when the
keeper himself wanted a light he had to
call for it. All lamps were out at the
proper time, and all chains were on every
person ; for the narrative says that, by the
earthquake, " Every man's bands were
loosed," which they could not be if they
were already unbound. The inmates were
all secured in their cells, and the whole
building was in due order. This shows
that the keeper of the prison attended to
his business thoroughly, nothing turning
him aside from the most correct observ-
ance of his instructions.

Well, all being shut up, he has gone to
bed, and is fast asleep, as he should be, in
the middle of the night, so as to be fit for
*his morning's work.* But what happens ?

" Paul and Silas, in their prison,
   Sang of Christ, the Lord arisen ;
   And an earthquake's arm of might
   Broke their dungeon gates at night."

See how every timber in the house quivers,
and he awakes out of his sleep.   What is
his first thought ?   To my mind it is fine
to observe that he has no terror for himself or family, but at once rushes from his
room to look to the prison below.   Seeing
the prison doors open, he was alarmed.
He does not seem to have been in any
alarm about his wife and his family,
though the earthquake must have shaken
the rooms in which they were, but his one
concern was his prison and its contents.
Under the seal and authority of the Roman emperor he was bound to keep the
prisoners safely, and when he wakes his
first thought concerns his duty.   I wish
that all Christians were as faithful in their
offices as this man !   When as yet he was
unenlightened, he was *faithful to those who
employed him.*   It is a grand thing when
a man, placed in an office of responsibility,
has his work so much upon his mind that
if he starts up in the middle of the night
and finds the floor under him reeling with
an earthquake, the main thing he thinks

about is the duty which he has engaged to fulfil. It ought to be so with Christian servants, with Christian trustees, managers, and confidential clerks, and indeed with all Christian men and women placed in offices of trust. Your chief concern should be to be found faithful; it was so with the jailor.

Now notice, as he finds the prison-doors open, this stern Roman *fears that he shall be disgraced*, for he feels sure that the prisoners must have fled. Naturally they would escape when the doors were open, and as he could not confront the charge of unfaithfulness in his office, he drew his sword in haste, and would have killed himself. For this proposed suicide he is to be most severely censured; but still note the stern Brutus-like fidelity of the man. He cannot endure the charge of having allowed his prisoners to escape, but would rather kill himself. Is it not singular that this Philippi was the place where Cassius committed suicide? where Brutus also slew himself? Here this man would have added another name to those who laid violent hands upon themselves, and all because he feared that he would lose his character. He preferred death to dishonour.   All these things show that he was a man sternly upright, and determined to perform his duty.   I am always doubly glad when such men are saved, because it does not often happen. Such persons too often wrap themselves up in the sense of having walked uprightly towards their fellow men, and because, after the lapse of many years they stand high in public esteem, and everybody says the country never had better servants, they are apt to forget their Master in heaven, and their obligations to their Lord—apt to have a blind eye towards their own shortcomings, and to be little inclined to sit as little children at the feet of Jesus, unless some wondrous deed of grace is wrought upon them.   Hence we admire the grace of God which brought such a man trembling to the apostle's feet.

The jailor was *a person of few words;* he was not a great talker, but a prompt actor.   We only know three things that he said.   First he called for a light, and next he cried, " Sirs, what must I do to be saved?" a terse, laconic question, respectful, earnest, to the point, having not a word too much or too little in it.   His other speech to Paul was of the same order when he said, "The magistrates have sent to let you go ; now, therefore, depart and go in peace." You would not expect a jailor to use very flowery language, he was accustomed to measure his syllables when he spoke to his prisoners, never uttering a word beyond the statute in that case made and provided. Thus he had acquired a hard business-like style of speech. Men of such a type are often cold as so many statues. We find it hard to warm their hearts, and therefore we bless the grace of God, which made this man's heart to burn within him and snapped the bonds of cold routine, so that, after his conversion, he feasted the ministers of Christ and rejoiced with all his house.

It may be well to make one more remark. It is evident that he was *a man of action, of precision and decision.* Once let him know what is to be done, and he does it. He acts as a man under authority having warders under him, he saith to this man, " Go, and he goeth ;" and he himself acts mechanically as his superiors command him. He was a man who, I suppose, opened the prison doors always to a minute at the right time in the morning for those who went out to exercise,

measured out the meals of the prisoners to
the ounce, and shut up the cells and put
out the lights exactly at the fixed hour
at night. I see it in him. Precise obedience is his main point. When he was
bidden to believe he believed; he was also
baptized straightway. What he lacked
in speech he made up in deeds. He
obeyed the Lord Jesus immediately, there
and then. I love to see a man brought to
Christ who has orderliness and decision
about him. Some of us are rough beings,
needing a deal of combing to bring us into
shape; but certain others are shapely
after their way from the first, and all that
they need is spiritual life. When the
divine life comes their habits are in beautiful consistency with the inward law of
obedience and holy order. Still, it is not
often that persons of this class are saved;
for these very orderly people frequently
think that they have no sin, and so the
warnings addressed to sinners do not
come home to them. For instance, a man
says, "Never since I took my position as
manager of my master's business have I
wasted an hour of his time, or a shilling of
his substance." This is well, but the devil
is ready with the suggestion, "Thou art a

good and faithful servant. What need hast thou to humble thyself before Christ, and seek mercy and grace?" It is a most blessed thing when this tendency is overcome. I see the divine splendour of grace as much in the conversion of the faultless moralist as in the repentance of Manasseh, or of that woman which was a sinner, of whom we spoke a little while ago. It is as hard to deliver a man from self-righteousness as from unrighteousness, as difficult to deliver one man from the frost-bite of his own orderliness as to save another from the heat of his unbridled passions. Converts like the jailor are very precious, and very sweetly display the love and power of God.

II. Now, secondly, WHAT OCCASIONED THE JAILOR'S CONVERSION? The narrative is short, and we cannot therefore get much out of it. I think, however, that we are warranted in believing that this man had received some measure of instruction before the earnest midnight cry of, "What must I do to be saved?" Perhaps the often re-peated testimony of the Pythoness had been reported to him, for it must have been a matter of general notoriety through-out the town of Philippi that this woman, who was supposed to be inspired, had testified that Paul and Silas were "servants of the Most High God." It is also very possible that when he was fitting on the irons to these holy men, and roughly thrusting them into the inner prison, their quiet manner, like sheep at the slaughter, and perhaps their godly words also, may have carried information to his mind. What he saw and heard did not savingly impress him, for he showed the apostles no sort of courtesy, but, as I have already said, was somewhat harsh with them. "He thrust them into the inner prison, and made their feet fast in the stocks:" so that at that time he had no belief in their mission, and but small respect for their character. He felt, it is clear, no compunction, for he went up to his chamber and fell asleep; nothing of any importance was on his mind notwithstanding what the apostles may have said to him. A young divine in a flowery sermon described the jailor as converted through hearing Paul and Silas sing at midnight. A very beautiful picture he made of it, but it had the drawback of being untrue, for the jailor did not hear them sing. "The prisoners heard them,"

for they were all down in the vaults under
the jailor's house; but it is clear that the
keeper of the prison did not hear them,
for he was asleep until the earthquake
startled him.

I have also heard it said that he was
converted through fear of death; a most
ridiculous remark, for how could he be
afraid to die who was going to kill himself? No, he was too brave a man to be
moved by terror. He was afraid of
nothing but of being suspected of neglect
of duty; he was a soldier without fear
and without reproach, dreading dishonour
infinitely more than death. He was a stern
disciplinarian, and thought little of his
own life or the lives of others. He would
have ridden in the charge of Balaclava,
with all the rest of them, bravely enough—

> "His not to reason why;
> His but to dare and die."

You can see that it was not fear that
brought him to the feet of the apostle.
I do not doubt that some are brought to
Christ by fear of death, but one is a
little suspicious of such conversions; for
he who is frightened to the Saviour by
fear of death may possibly run away from

him when he perceives that his fear has no immediate cause.

Others, too, have thought that he was made to tremble because he was afraid of being brought before Cæsar for permitting his prisoners to escape. That fear may have hurried him into the desperate intent of suicide, but it was not the cause of his conversion, for all distress upon that point was gone before he cried out, "Sirs, what must I do to be saved?" In fact, he came to Paul and Silas because that fear had been banished by hearing the calm and brave voice of the apostle as he said, "Do thyself no harm : we are all here." It was not even a fear of censure from the magistrates which compelled him to tremble, for that also had been removed by finding the prisoners still in their cells ; and, though the whole of these things together make up the circumstances of his conversion they cannot be put down as the cause of it, since this last especially had ceased to operate upon him when he fell trembling at the apostle's feet.

What was it, then, which led to the jailor's faith and baptism? I answer, partly the miracle that the doors were opened and the prisoners' bonds loosed by an earthquake; and coupled with that the fact that none of them had escaped. What gladness filled his bosom! He would not be arraigned after all for being unfaithful to his trust. How strange that the prisoners were all there. What a conflict was there in his spirit! What anxiety, and what sudden quelling of his alarm! There was no need to commit suicide lest he should be blamed, for there was nothing for which to blame him. What a deliverance for him! An awful power was abroad, and yet it had taken care of him. A mingled feeling of mystery and gladness created astonishment and gratitude in his bosom. He could not make it out, it was so singular: he had been brought to the verge of a precipice, and yet was safe. "Do thyself no harm; we are all here," rang out like music in his ear. He felt a solemn awe of those two prisoners whose voice had reassured him. Their voice had been to him as the very voice of God sounding forth along those corridors out of the innermost cells. Their bold, truthful, confident, calm tones had astonished him. He had seen before something very singular about those two men, but now the very tone in which they conveyed to him the glad intelligence which banished his worst fear filled him with deep reverence towards them: and he feels that no doubt these men are the servants of the Most High God, and therefore he calls for a light, breaks in upon their darkness, and brings them out.

While this was transpiring, he was brought very near to the world to come by the fact of the sword having been so near his breast, by the earthquake that had started all the stones of the dungeon, by the singular power of God miraculously holding every free man as fast as if he had been bound, and by the presence of men whom he perceived to be linked with deity. This nearness to things unseen caused him to look over his past life. He was calm despite the confusion of the night, for he was not a man to be frightened; but conscience, which in him was quick and prompt from the very habit of obedience, reviewed his past life, judged it and condemned it, and he felt that he was a lost man because of his multiplied shortcomings before the living God, whose servants were there present. For this reason he cried out, "Sirs, what must I do to be saved?" It was none other than

the blessed and eternal Spirit, unfolding
before him his life which he had thought
to be so correct, making him to see the
evil of it, and striking him down with a
sense of guilt and a dread of consequent
punishment. So far we trace his convic-
tions to an awakened conscience visited
by the Spirit of God.

His full conversion grew out of the
further instructions of the apostles. That
answer was very like his short question in
fulness of meaning : " Believe on the Lord
Jesus Christ, and thou shalt be saved, and
thy house." This was condensed gospel
for him ; and then followed a blessed
commentary upon it, when the apostle
spoke the word of the Lord both to him
and to all his house ; all this lit up
his mind which was already willing to receive the truth, a mind which, from the
very habit of obedience, was quick and
prompt to accept the sway of the Lord
Jesus. He received the word in the love
of it most sweetly, God the Holy Spirit
blessing it to him while he listened.
There was plain teaching, and a simple
heart to receive it, and the two together
made quick work of it, and made re-
splendent that strange midnight which

was henceforth in that house regarded as the beginning of days.

Now, dear friend, I want you to thank God for the circumstances which surround any man's conversion, for all things are well ordered. If the Lord has been pleased to call you by his grace, do not begin judging your conversion because the circumstances were not very remarkable, and do not suspect your friend's sincerity because there was no earthquake in connection with his new birth, for the Lord may not be in the earthquake, nor in the wind, nor in the fire, but in that "still small voice" which calls the heart to Jesus. The matter is not how you came to Christ, but are you there? It is not *what* brought you so much as *who* brought you. Did the Spirit of God lead you to repentance, and are you resting at the cross? If so, then, whether, like Lydia, your heart was gently opened, or, like this jailor, you were startled and awakened, and thus made to perceive grand truths to which you had been a stranger before, it does not matter so long as Christ is believed in and your heart yields itself to his blessed sway.

III. Our third point—and may the

Spirit of God help us in it—is to notice
WHAT SORT OF CONVERT THIS MAN MADE.

First, you are quite sure he made a very
*believing* convert. The gospel command
came to him—" Believe in the Lord Jesus
Christ, and thou shalt be saved, and
thy house"; and he did believe, believed
firmly, without raising questions or dis-
cussions, without delays, or hesitations.
How many there are among those whose
conversion we seek after, who meet us always with a "but." We put the truth
plainly, and they reply, "Yes—but—."
Then we go over it again, and put it
in another shape, and they still say "but."
We tell them that salvation is by believing in Jesus Christ, and they answer
"*but.*" This man, however, had no "*buts.*"
He was told to believe and he did believe,
and who would not who knows how true
the gospel is? Who will not believe what
is true? Who will not rely upon that
which is divinely certified? Why should
we reject what thousands have proved to
be true by a gladsome experience? Ah,
unbelief, what an enemy thou art to multitudes who hear the gospel! But thou
wast utterly cast out of the jailor: he
heard the command to believe, and, though

he had received slender instruction, he nevertheless believed unto eternal life. He was a convert full of faith.

Next, what a *humble* Christian he was. He fell down at the feet of the servants of God, not feeling himself worthy to stand in their presence ; and then, though their jailor, he took them up into his house and waited upon them with gladness. The man who is really born again does not demand the best seat in the synagogue, nor disdain to perform the meanest service. It is poor evidence of a renewed heart when a man must always be the forehorse in the team, or else he will do nothing at all. He who knows the Lord loves to sit at Christ's feet : the lower the place the better for him. He is glad even to wash the saints' feet, yea, he thinks it an honour. If you, Christian people, must dispute about precedence always fight for the lowest place. If you aspire to be last and least you will not have many competitors ; there will be no need to demand a poll, for the lowest seat is undisputed. Humility is the way to a peaceful life, and the jailor began to practise it in his behaviour to his prisoners, who were now his pastors.

What a *ready* convert he was! In that
one midnight he passed through several
stages : hearing, believing, baptizing, service, rejoicing and fellowship, and all
within an hour. No long waiting for
him! I wish more converts were like
him. What slow-coaches we have to
deal with. You travel by broad-wheeled
wagon to heaven, even you who rush along
by express train in the world's business.
Yes, you must attend to the world, and
my Lord and Master may wait your con-
venience, as Felix put it ; but this should
not be. As soon as you know what your
Lord would have you to do, every moment
of unnecessary delay is a sin. The jailor
had been prompt in other duties, and he
was just as decided with regard to divine
things : he was such a convert as we like
to have in our churches, to set an example
of quick obedience to the Great Captain
of our salvation. Soldierly habits sancti-
fied by grace are greatly needed in the
church of God ; would God we saw more
of them.

Then, see, what a *practical* convert he
was! "He took them the same hour of
the night and washed their stripes, and
set meat before them." All that he could

do he did at once, and his wife and children were all busy to help him.    It is not easy to fit up a feast in the middle of the night, but the good wife did her best ; cold meats were brought forth from the stores, and such good cheer as they had was set out, so that the two good men, who, no doubt, needed refreshment, were sufficiently supplied.    I think I see that midnight festival even now.    How the young children caught up every word which was spoken by the holy men, and how glad they were to see them at their table !    They all believed and were all baptized, and therefore they were all eager to do something for the men of God.    How pleased they were to fetch the good men up into the best parlour,—how eager to put them into the easiest chairs and let them sit in comfort, or recline at their ease.    They did not wait till morning, but showed kindness without delay.    This is the sort of convert the church needs : one who delights to serve the Lord, and is no sooner converted than he sets to work in his own hearty way.    May the Lord send us scores of such conversions !

Friend, have you ever done anything for the Lord or his cause ?  "No, sir.  Nobody has set me anything to do." What, live in these busy times, and want somebody to find you Christian employment! Why, you are not worth setting to work! He who lives in a great city and cannot find something to do for God, had better not get off his knees till he has asked his Lord to have mercy upon his lazy soul. Here are people dying all round us, and being lost for ever, through ignorance and drunkenness and sin of every kind, and yet a young man of one-and-twenty stands up and says that he cannot find anything to do! You are idle. You are very idle. Does not Solomon say, "Whatsoever thy hand findeth to do, do it with thy might"? you need not open your eyes to find good work to do, only put out your hand and there it is. For the love of Jesus, begin to serve him as this jailor and his wife and family did.

Notice again that they were very *joyful* converts. He "rejoiced, believing in God with all his house." The apostle was happy that night. His poor back was smarting, but his heart was leaping within him; and Silas too, who had shared the scourging, he also shared the joy. How lovingly the jailor looked upon his

**two** instructors, how tenderly he washed their stripes. As he had thrown them into the inner prison, so he brought them into his own house. What overflowing joy was in his heart! Methinks while he was waiting at the table he would every now and then stop and wonder at what grace had done. Would he not ask the apostle to teach him that psalm which had been sung below stairs? I am sure he would have sung heartily had he known that hymn which you so much delight in, wherein each one declares,

"I am so glad that Jesus loves me."

Joy ruled at that midnight feast, and well it might, for the prison had become a palace, and the jailor an heir of heaven.

This man was an *influential* convert, for through his conversion, all his house was led to believe; and he was also a *sensible* convert, which is worth notice, for it is not every Christian man that is wise and prudent. Some zealous people are in a hurry to give up their secular callings. Such would say, "I cannot be a jailor any longer. I must give it up." A Roman jailor would have much to do which would grate upon Christian

feelings, but there was nothing positively
wrong in the office.  Somebody must be
jailor, and who so fit for the post as a man
who knows the Lord and will therefore
manifest a gentle, humane spirit?  Who
so fit to have poor creatures entrusted
to him as one who will not swear at them,
or treat them roughly, but who will seek
their good ?  Why, methinks, if a man
wanted to be a missionary to those who
needed him most, he might desire to be a
jailor, for he would be sure to get at the
very people who most require the gospel.
The Philippian convert was in his right
place, and instead of saying, "Ah, I must
give up my situation, and live with Christian people," he was wise enough to stay
at the jail, and abide in his calling.  Observe that when the magistrates tell him
that Paul is to go he does not violate
their order out of zeal for the faith.  He
had no right to keep Paul as a guest in
his house against the magistrates' will, or
he would gladly have retained him ; but
being bound by his office and by the fact
that his apartments were part of the jail,
when Paul was bidden to go, he said to him,
" Now, therefore, go in peace."  The words
look somewhat curt, but no doubt he

uttered them in such a kind and courteous manner that the apostle quite understood him. Then Paul went down to Lydia's house, and I dare say the jailor came down to see him there; so that if they could not meet at the jail without breach of regulations, they could meet at Lydia's hospitable abode. He was quite right in maintaining the discipline of the jail and his sincere affection for the apostle at the same time.

My own belief is that he and Lydia were ever afterwards two of the kindest friends that the apostle ever had, and were chief among those who contributed of their substance to his necessities. Paul took no money from any but the Philippians. Though other churches offered to contribute, Paul declined; but when the Philippians sent to him once and again, he accepted their gifts as a sacrifice of sweet smell. He said within himself, "All the family send this gift; all Lydia's household and all the jailor's household are believers, so that no member of the family will grudge what is sent to me." One likes to see brought into the Christian church those who will continue in their business and make money for Jesus Christ, and lay themselves out to serve the Lord in a practical fashion. Many a man gets into a pulpit and spoils a congregation who, if he had stuck to his business and made money that he might help the poor or aid the cause of missions or support the church of God, would have been more truly serving the great cause. He was a sensible convert, this jailor, and I rejoice in him.

And now, if I have been addressing anybody not a jailor, but a person in a position of trust, and if you have a feeling that you have done faithfully, I am glad of it. I am not going to dispute your claim to integrity towards man, nor to undervalue honesty and faithfulness; but oh, remember, you need to be saved. Notwithstanding your moral excellence you will be lost unless you believe in the Lord Jesus Christ. Do see to this. May the Holy Spirit lead you at once to accept the gospel of grace, for you need it even as others. May you become a firm believer in Jesus, and may the Church find in you a willing and earnest helper.

# ONESIMUS;

## OR,

## THE RUNAWAY SERVANT

"I beseech thee for my son Onesimus, whom I have begotten in my bonds: which in time past was to thee unprofitable, but now profitable to thee and to me: whom I have sent again: thou therefore receive him, that is, mine own bowels: whom I would have retained with me, that in thy stead he might have ministered unto me in the bonds of the gospel: but without thy mind would I do nothing; that thy benefit should not be as it were of necessity, but willingly. For perhaps he therefore departed for a season, that thou shouldest receive him for ever; not now as a servant, but above a servant, a brother beloved, specially to me, but how much more unto thee, both in the flesh and in the Lord?"—Philemon 10—16.

ONESIMUS was a runaway servant in Rome, but he had been converted under Paul's preaching in that great city, and henceforth the apostle regarded him as his own son. I do not know why Onesimus when he reached Rome found his way to Paul. Perhaps he went to him as a great many scapegraces have come to me —because their fathers or relatives knew me; and so, as Onesimus's master had known Paul, the servant applied to his master's friend, perhaps to beg some little help in his extremity. Anyhow, Paul seized the opportunity and preached the gospel to him, and the runaway slave became a believer in the Lord Jesus Christ. Paul watched him, admired the character of his convert, was glad to be served by him, and became intensely attached to him. When he thought it right that he should return to his master, Philemon, he took a deal of trouble to compose a letter of apology for him, which we now call "the Epistle to Philemon." Paul, as you know, was not accustomed to write letters with his own hand, but dictated to an amanuensis. It is supposed that he had an affection of the eyes, and therefore when he did write he used large capital letters, for he says in one of his shorter epistles, "Ye see how large a letter I have written unto you with my own hand." The letter to Philemon, at least, part of it, was not dictated, but was written by his own hand. See the eighteenth and nineteenth verses—" If he have wronged thee, or oweth thee ought, put that on mine account; I Paul have written it with mine own hand, I will repay it." It is the only note of hand which I recollect in Scripture, but there it is—an I O U for whatever amount Onesimus may have stolen.

Let us cultivate a large-hearted spirit, and sympathise with new converts when we find them in trouble through past wrong-doing. It is not ours to say that it serves them right, but to see how we can extricate them from their difficulties. Let us try and set the fallen ones on their feet again, and give them, as we say, "a fair start in the world." If God has forgiven them, surely we may, and if Jesus Christ has received them they cannot be too bad for us to receive. Let us do for them what Jesus would have done had he been here, so shall we truly be the disciples of Jesus.

Thus I introduce the text, and we notice concerning it, first, that it contains *a singular instance of divine grace*. Secondly, it brings before us *a case of sin overruled*. And, thirdly, it may be regarded as *an example of relationship improved by grace*.

for now Onesimus, who had been a slave
for a season, would abide with Philemon
all his lifetime, and be no more a servant
but a brother beloved.

I. First, let us look at Onesimus as AN
INSTANCE OF DIVINE GRACE.

We see the grace of God in his *election*.
He was a slave. In those days slaves
were very ignorant, untaught, and degraded. Being barbarously used, they
were for the most part themselves sunk in
the lowest barbarism, neither did their
masters attempt to raise them out of it.
It is possible that Philemon's endeavour
to do good to Onesimus may have been
irksome to the man, and he may therefore
have fled from his house. His master's
prayers, warnings, and Christian regulations may have been disagreeable to him,
and therefore he ran away. He wronged
his master, which he could scarcely have
done if he had not been treated to some
extent as a confidential servant. Possibly
the unusual kindness of Philemon, and
the trust he reposed in his slave may have
been too much for his untrained nature.
We know not what he stole, but evidently
he had taken something, for the apostle
says, "If he hath wronged thee, or oweth

thee ought, put that on mine account."
He ran away from Colosse, therefore, and,
thinking that he would be less likely to
be discovered by the ministers of justice,
he sought the city of Rome, which was
then as large as London now is, and perhaps larger. There in those back slums
of the Jews' quarter Onesimus could hide;
or he would obtain shelter amongst those
gangs of thieves which infested the im-
perial city. He thought that he would
not be known or be heard of any more,
and could live the free and easy life of one
who has no ties, and no particular calling.
Yet, mark you, the Lord looked out of
heaven with an eye of love, and set that
eye on Onesimus. Oh that he may look
on any reckless youth who has left his
father's house because he cannot bear the
just restraints of the parental rule.

Were there no free men, that God must
elect a slave? Were there no faithful
servants, that he must choose one who had
embezzled his master's money? Were there
none of the educated and polite, that he
must needs look upon a barbarian? Were
there none among the moral and the excellent, that infinite love should fix itself
upon this degraded being, who was now

mixed up with the very scum of society?
And what the scum of society was in old
Rome I should not like to think. The
upper classes were about as brutalised in
their general habits as we can very well
conceive ; and what the lowest must have
been, none of us can tell. Bad as we now
are, society is by no means so unutterably
vile in its habits as in the days of Nero
and Caligula : indeed, men would not
tolerate in the most filthy haunts of vice
the deeds which were then done openly by
all ranks. The world was deeply depraved,
and Onesimus was among the worst of the
worst ; and yet eternal love, which passed
by kings and princes, and left Pharisees
and Sadducees, philosophers and magi, to
stumble in the dark, fixed its eye upon
this poor benighted creature that he might
be made a vessel unto honour, fit for the
Master's use.

This is ever the way of grace, it glories
in selecting those whom human partiality
would have passed by, that it may abase the
pride of man and reveal the sovereignty
of God.

"I will have mercy on whom I will
have mercy, and I will have compassion
on whom I will have compassion," are

sentences which roll like thunder alike from the cross of Calvary and from the mount of Sinai. The Lord is a sovereign, and doeth as he pleases. Let us admire that marvellous electing love which selected such a one as Onesimus!

Grace also is to be observed, in the next place, in the *conversion* of this runaway slave.

Look at him! How unlikely he appears to become a convert. He was an Asiatic slave of about the same grade as an ordinary Lascar, or "heathen Chinee." He was, however, worse than the ordinary Lascar, who is certainly free, and probably an honest man, if he is nothing else : this man was a slave and a thief, and was without home or family, for after taking his master's property he had left all the associations of the town in which he had been brought up, and had run away to Rome. He was like a derelict vessel, without owner or helmsman, drifting to sure destruction, with no man to care what became of him. But everlasting love means to convert the man, and converted he shall be. He had probably heard Paul preach at Colosse, but he had not been impressed by the word. At Rome, Paul

was not preaching in St. Peter's: it
was in no such noble building, but it was
probably down there at the back of the
Palatine hill, where the prætorian guard
had their lodgings, and where there was
a military prison called the Prætorium.
In a bare room in the barrack prison Paul
sat with a soldier chained to his hand,
preaching to all who were admitted to hear
him, and there it was that the grace of God
reached the heart of the wild runaway, the
embezzler of his master's goods. What a
change it made in him immediately! Now
you see him repenting of his sin, grieved
to think he has wronged a good master,
vexed at his own folly, and confounded as
he beholds the depravity of his heart as
well as the error of his life. He weeps as
Paul preaches of judgment to come: the
glance of joy is in his eye as he hears of
redeeming love: and from that heavy heart
a load is taken. New thoughts light up his
dark mind; his heart is relieved from
despair, his face is changed, and the entire
man renewed, for the grace of God has in
his case turned the lion to a lamb, the
raven to a dove.

Some of us, I have no doubt, are quite
as wonderful instances of divine election and

effectual calling as Onesimus was. Let us, therefore, record the lovingkindness of the Lord, and let us say to ourselves, " Christ shall have the glory of it. The Lord hath done it; and unto the Lord be honour, world without end."

The grace of God was conspicuous *in the character which it wrought in Onesimus* upon his conversion, for he appears to have been helpful, useful, and profitable. So Paul says. Paul was willing to have had him as an associate, and this is greatly in his favour; it is not every man that is converted that we should altogether choose as a companion. There are odd people to be met with who will go to heaven we have no doubt, for they are pilgrims on the right way, but we have no wish for much of their company on the road. They are cross-grained, crabbed, and cantankerous, with a something about them that one's nature can no more delight in than the palate can take pleasure in nauseous physic. They are a sort of spiritual hedgehogs; they are alive and useful, and no doubt they illustrate the wisdom and patience of God, but they are not good companions: one would not like to carry them in his bosom. But Onesimus was evidently of a kind, tender, loving spirit. Paul called him, "my son Onesimus, whom I have begotten in my bonds," and even says, "Receive him, that is, mine own bowels." He said that he would have retained him that he might have ministered to him in the bonds of the gospel, had he not thought it better to have his master's full consent first. When Paul bade him return, was it not a clear proof of change of heart in Onesimus that he would go back? Away as he was in Rome he might have passed on from one town to another, have avoided the authorities, and have remained perfectly free; but feeling that he was under obligation to his master—especially since he had injured him—he takes Paul's advice and returns to his old position. He will go back, and take a letter of apology or introduction to his master, for he feels that it is his duty to make reparation for the wrong he has done. A resolve to make restitution of former wrongs is a test of sincerity in people who profess to be converted. If they have taken money or goods wrongfully they ought to repay it; it were well if they returned sevenfold. If we have in any way robbed or wronged another, the first instincts of grace in the heart will suggest compensation in all ways within our power. Do not think it is to be got over by saying, "God has forgiven me, and therefore I may leave it." No, dear friend ; but inasmuch as God has forgiven you, try to undo all the wrong, and prove the sincerity of your repentance by restitution. So Onesimus was content to go back to Philemon, and work out his term of years with him, or do as Philemon wishes, for though he might have preferred to wait upon Paul, his service was due to the man whom he had injured. That showed a gentle, humble, honest, upright spirit ; and let Onesimus be commended for it : nay, let the grace of God be extolled for it. Look at the difference between the man who robbed his master and ran away and the new man who came back of his own accord to be profitable to the master he had defrauded.

What wonders the grace of God has done ! What wonders the grace of God can do ! Many plans are employed in the world for the reformation of the wicked and the reclaiming of the fallen, and to every one of these, as far as they are rightly bottomed, we wish good success; for whatsoever things are lovely, and pure, and of good report, we wish them God speed. But mark this word,—the true reforming of the drunkard lies in giving him a new heart: and the real reclaiming of the harlot is to be found in a renewed nature. Let others do what they will, but God forbid that I should glory save in the cross of our Lord Jesus Christ. I see certain of my brethren fiddling away at the branches of the tree of vice with their wooden saws; but, as for the gospel, it lays the axe at the root of every tree in the whole forest of evil, and if it be fairly received into the heart it fells all the upas trees at once, and causes instead of them the fir tree, the pine tree, and the box tree together, to spring up and flourish, to beautify the house of our Master's glory. Let us, since we see what the Spirit of God can do for men, publish abroad the gospel of the grace of God, and extol the Lord with all our might.

II. And now, secondly, we have in our text, and its connection, a very interesting INSTANCE OF SIN OVERRULED.

Onesimus had no right to rob his master and run away; but God was pleased to make use of that crime for his conversion. His dishonesty drove him to Rome, and so led him to the spot where Paul was preaching, and thus it brought him to Christ, and to his right mind. Now, when we speak of this, we must be cautious, lest we seem to excuse the guilt which incidentally led up to the great blessing. When Paul says, "Perhaps he departed for a season, that thou shouldest receive him for ever," he does not apologize for the absconding of Onesimus, but he generously suggests a reason for his master's forgiving him the wrong. He does not make it out that Onesimus did right—not for a moment. Sin is sin, and, whatever it may be overruled to do, yet sin is still evil and only evil. The crucifixion of our Saviour has brought the greatest conceivable blessings upon mankind, yet none the less it was "with wicked hands" that they took Jesus and crucified him. The selling of Joseph into Egypt was the means in the hand of God of the preservation of Jacob, and his sons, in the time of famine; but his brethren were none the less guilty for having sold him for a slave. Let it always be remembered that the faultiness or virtue of an act is not contingent upon the result of that act. If, for instance, a man who has been set on a

railway to turn the switch forgets to do it,
you call it a very great crime if the train
comes to mischief and a dozen people are
killed.  Yes, but the crime is the same if
nobody is killed.  It is not the result of
the carelessness, but the carelessness itself
which deserves punishment.  If it were
the man's duty to turn the switch in such-
and-such a way, and his not doing so
should even by some strange accident
turn to the saving of life, the man would
be equally blameworthy.  There would
be no credit due to him for good results,
for if his duty lies in a certain line his
fault also lies in a certain line, namely,
the neglecting of that duty.  So if God
overrules sin for good, as he sometimes
does, it is none the less sin; only there
is so much the more glory to the wonderful wisdom and grace of God who, out
of evil, brings forth good.  Onesimus is
not excused, then, for having enbezzled
his master's goods, nor for havng left
him without right; he is still a transgressor, but God's grace is glorified.

Remember, too, that when Onesimus
left his master he was performing an action
the results of which, in all probbility,
would have been ruinous to himsel.  He

was living as a trusted dependent beneath the roof of a kind master, who had a church in his house. If I read the epistle rightly, he had a godly mistress and a godly master, and he had an opportunity of learning the gospel continually; but this reckless young blade, very likely, could not bear it, and could have lived more contentedly with a heathen master, who would have beaten him one day and made him drunk another. He threw away the opportunities of salvation, and went to Rome, and he doubtless went into the lowest part of the city, and associated, as I have already told you, with the most depraved company. Now, had it come to pass that he had joined in the insurrections of the slaves which took place frequently about that time, as he in all probability would have done had not grace prevented, he would have been put to death as others had been. Short shrift was given to rebel slaves in Rome: half suspect a man, and off with his head was the rule towards slaves and vagabonds. Onesimus was just the very man that would have been likely to be hurried to death and to eternal destruction. When a young man suddenly leaves home and goes to London, we know what that means. When his friends do not know where he is, and he does not want them to know, we are aware, within a little, where he is and what he is at. What Onesimus was doing I do not know, but he was certainly doing his best to ruin himself. His course, therefore, is to be judged, as far as he is concerned, by what it was likely to bring him to; and though it did not bring him to ruin, that was no credit to him, but all the honour of his rescue was due to the overruling power of God.

See how God overruled all. Thus had the Lord purposed. Nobody shall be able to touch the heart of Onesimus but Paul. Onesimus is living at Colosse; Paul cannot come there, he is in prison. It is needful, then, that Onesimus should be brought to Paul. Suppose the kindness of Philemon's heart had prompted him to say to Onesimus, "I want you to go to Rome, and find Paul out and hear him." This naughty servant would have said, "I am not going to risk my life to hear a sermon. If I go with a letter I shall deliver it, but I want none of his preaching." Sometimes, when persons are brought to hear a preacher, with the view of their being

converted, if they have any idea that such
is the object, it is about the last thing
likely to happen, because they resolve to
be fire-proof against the gospel, and so
the preaching does not come home to
them: and it would, probably, have been
so with Onesimus. No, no, he was not to
be won in that way, he must be drawn to
Rome by some other method. How shall
it be done? Well, the devil shall do it, not
knowing that he will be losing a willing
servant thereby. The devil tempts Onesimus to steal. Onesimus yields to the
temptation, and then, fearful of being discovered, he makes tracks for Rome as
quickly as he can, and gets down among
the back slums, and there he feels what the
prodigal felt—a hungry belly, which to
many is one of the best preachers in the
world: their conscience is reached through
their being made to feel the result of their
wrong-doing. Being very hungry, not
knowing what to do, and no man giving
anything to him, he considers whether
there is anybody in Rome that would pity
him. He does not know a single person in
the city, and is likely to starve. Perhaps
one morning a Christian woman was going
to hear Paul, and seeing this poor man

fainting upon the steps of a temple, she went to him and spoke about his soul. "Soul," said he, "I care nothing about that, but my body would thank you for something to eat. I am starving." She replied, "Come with me, then," and she gave him bread, and as she did so she said, "I do this for Jesus Christ's sake." "Jesus Christ!" he said, "I have heard of him. I used to hear of him over at Colosse." "Whom did you hear speak of him?" the woman would ask. "Why, a short man, with weak eyes, a great preacher, named Paul, who used to come to my master's house." "Why, I am going to hear him preach," the woman would say, "will you go with me?" "Yes, I think I should like to see the man again. He always had a kind word to say to the poor." So he goes in and pushes his way among the soldiers, and Paul's Master incites the apostle to speak the right word. It may have been so, or it may have been the other way—that not knowing anybody else, he remembered that Paul was there a prisoner, and went to the prison to ask his help. He goes down to the Præ-torium and finds him there, tells him of his extreme poverty, and Paul reasons with

him and so he becomes a Christian. It
may have been in either of these ways
that the man's heart was won; at any
rate, the Lord must have Onesimus in
Rome to hear Paul, and the sin of
Onesimus, though perfectly voluntary on
his part, so that God had no hand in it,
was yet overruled by a mysterious providence to bring him where the gospel was
blest to his soul.

Now, I want to speak to some of you
Christian people about this matter. Have
you a son who has left home? Is he a
wilful, wayward young man, who has gone
away because he could not bear the restraints of a Christian family? It is a
sad thing it should be so—a very sad
thing, but do not despond, much less
despair about him. You do not know
where he is, but God does; and you cannot follow him, but the Spirit of God can.
He is going a voyage to Shanghai. Ah,
there may be a Paul at Shanghai who is
to be the means of his salvation, and as
that Paul is not in England your son,
must go there. Is it to Australia that he
is sailing? There may be a word spoken
there by the blessing of God to your son,
which is the only word that will ever reach

him. I cannot speak it, nobody in London can speak it; but a man in the far-off land will be directed to do so; and God, therefore, is letting your boy go away in all his wilfulness and folly that he may be brought under the means of grace, which will prove effectual to his salvation. Many a sailor boy has been wild, reckless, Godless, Christless, and at last has got into a foreign hospital. Ah, if his mother knew that he was down with the yellow fever, how sad her mind would be, for she would conclude that her dear son will die away from home, and that she will not even have the mournful privilege of weeping over his grave. Yet, perhaps, the mother's fears are all groundless, for it is just in that hospital that God means to save her boy. A sailor writes to me somewhat as follows. He says, "My mother asked me to read a chapter of the Bible every day, but I never did. I got into the hospital at Havannah, and, when I lay there, a man near to me was dying; but before he departed he said to me, 'Mate, could you come here? I want to speak to you. I have got something here that is very precious to me. I was a wild fellow, but reading this packet of sermons

has brought me to the Saviour, and
I am dying with a good hope through
grace. Now, when I am dead and gone,
will you take these sermons and read them,
and may God bless them to you. And
will you write a letter to the man who
preached those sermons, to tell him that
through them I have learned to die in
peace.'" It was a packet of my sermons, and God was pleased to make them
useful to that young man, so that he became a Christian. I have no doubt whatever that he was sent to the hospital by a
gracious providence that there he might
receive the books which the Holy Spirit
would employ in his regeneration. You do
not know, dear mother, you do not know
the deep designs of divine grace. The
worst thing that can occur to a young man
is sometimes the best thing that can happen to him. I have sometimes thought,
when I have seen young men of position
and wealth taking to racing and all sorts
of dissipation, "Well, it is a dreadfully
bad thing, but it may by a roundabout
process lead to repentance. They will get
through their money very quickly, and
when they have come down to beg-
gary, they will be like the young gentle-

man in the parable who returned to his father because he could not live away from him. " When he had spent all, there arose a mighty famine in that land, and he began to be in want. And he said, I will arise and go to my father." Perhaps the disease which often follows upon vice—perhaps the poverty which comes like an armed man after extravagance and debauch—is but love in another form, sent to compel the sinner to come to himself and consider his ways, and seek the ever-merciful God.

You Christian people often see the little gutter children—the poor little arabs in the street, and you feel much pity for them, as well you may ; but I have often thought that the poverty and hunger of these poor little children has a louder voice to most hearts than their vice and ignorance. God knew that we were not ready and able to hear the cry of the child's soul, and so he added the child's hunger of body to that cry, that he might pierce our hearts. People could live in sin, and be happy after their own poor fashion, if they were well-to-do and rich ; and if sin did not make parents poor and wretched, and their children miserable, we should not so clearly see it, and therefore we should not arouse ourselves to grapple with it. It is a benefit in some diseases when the patient can throw the complaint out upon the skin: and oftentimes outward sin and outward misery are a sort of throwing out of the disease of natural depravity, so that the eye of those who know where the healing medicine is to be had is thereby drawn to the mischief, and the soul's secret malady is dealt with. Onesimus might have stopped at home, and he might never have been a thief, and yet he might have been lost through self-righteousness. But now he has absconded his sin is visible. The scapegrace has displayed the depravity of his heart, and now it is that he comes under Paul's eye and Paul's prayer, and becomes converted. Do not, I pray you, ever despair of man or woman or child because you see their sin upon the surface of their character. On the contrary, say to yourself, " This is placed where I can see it, that I may pray about it. It is made sadly visible to my eye, that I may the more earnestly concern myself to bring this poor soul to Jesus Christ, the mighty Saviour, who can save the most forlorn sinner." Look at vice with the eye of earnest, active benevolence, and rouse yourselves to conquer it. Our duty is to hope on and to pray on so long as life lingers in the object of our prayer. We cannot tell the designs of God, but we may rest assured that believing prayer cannot fail. Perhaps the boy has been so wayward that his sin may come to a crisis, and a new heart may be given him. Perhaps your daughter's evil has been developed that the Lord may convince her of sin and bring her to the Saviour's feet. At any rate, if the case be ever so bad, hope in God and pray on.

III. Once more. Our text may be viewed as AN EXAMPLE OF RELATIONS IMPROVED. "He therefore departed for a season, that thou shouldest receive him for ever; *not now as a servant, but a brother beloved, specially to me, but how much more unto thee?*" We are a long while learning great truths. Perhaps Philemon had not found out that it was wrong for him to hold a slave. Some men who were very good in their time did not know the sin of it. John Newton did not know that he was doing wrong by engaging in the slave trade, and George Whitefield, when he left slaves, which had been willed to him, to the orphanage of Savannah, did not think for a moment that he was doing anything more than if he had been dealing with horses, or gold and silver. Public sentiment was not enlightened, although the gospel has always struck at the very root of slavery. The essence of gospel precept is that we are to do to others as we would that they should do to us, and nobody would wish to be another man's slave, and therefore he has no right to hold another man in bondage. Perhaps when Onesimus ran away and came back again, this letter of Paul may have opened Philemon's eyes as to his own position. He may have been an excellent master, and have trusted his servant, and treated him not as a slave, but as a confidential servant; but perhaps he had not regarded him as a brother man; and now Onesimus has come back he will be a better servant, but Philemon will also be a better master, and a slave-holder no longer. He will regard his former servant as a brother in Christ. Now, this is what the grace of God does when it comes into a family. It does not alter the relations; it does not give the child a right to be pert, and

refuse obedience to his parents; it does not
give the father a right to lord it over his
family without wisdom and love, for it
tells him that he is not to provoke his
children to anger, lest they be discouraged; it does not give the servant
the right to be a master, neither does it
take away from the master his position, or
allow him to exaggerate his authority, but
all round it softens and sweetens. Row-
land Hill used to say that he would not
give a halfpenny for a man's piety if his
dog and his cat were not better off after
he was converted. There was much weight
in that remark. Everything in the house
goes better when grace oils the wheels.
The mistress is, perhaps, naturally rather
sharp, quick, tart; but her constitution is
marvellously sweetened when she receives
the grace of God. The servant may be apt
to loiter, may be late up of a morning,
very slovenly, fond of a gossip at the door;
but, if she is truly converted, all that kind
of thing comes to an end. She is con-
scientious, and attends to her duty as she
ought. The master, when he is a truly
Christian man, has gentleness, suavity,
and considerateness about him. The husband is the head of the wife, but when

renewed by grace he is a very loving head.
The wife also keeps her place, and seeks
by gentleness and wisdom to make the
house as happy as she can. I do not believe in your religion, dear friend, if it
belongs to the chapel and the prayer-
meeting, and not to your home. The best
religion in the world is that which smiles
at the table, works at the sewing machine,
and is pleasant in the chimney-corner and
amiable in the drawing-room. Give me
the religion which blacks boots, and shines
them well; cooks the food so that it can
be eaten; measures out yards of calico,
and does not make them half-an-inch
short; sells a hundred yards of an article,
and does not label ninety as a hundred,
as many tradespeople do. That is true
Christianity which affects the whole of
life. If we are truly Christians we shall
be changed in our relationships to our
fellow men, and hence we shall regard
those whom we call our inferiors with
quite a different eye. It is wrong in Christian people when they are so sharp upon
little faults that they see in servants,
especially if they are Christian servants.
That is not the way to correct them. Some
mistresses see a little something wrong,

and they are down upon the poor girls,
as if they had been guilty of murder or
high treason. If your Master, and mine,
were to treat us in that style, I wonder
how long we should be found in his service. How quick some are in discharging
their maids for small errors. No excuse,
no trying her again : she must go, and
where she goes is no concern of ours.
Is this doing as a Christian should do?
Many a young man has been turned out of
a situation for the veriest trifle by a Christian employer, who must have known that
he would expose his servant to all sorts of
risks; and many a domestic has been sent
adrift as if she were a dog, with no sort of
thought whether another position could
be found, and without anything being
done to prevent her going astray. Do let
us think of others, especially of those
whom Christ loves even as he does us.
Philemon might have said, "No, no, I
don't take you back, Mr. Onesimus, not
I. Once bit, twice shy, sir. I never ride
a broken-kneed horse. You stole my
money; I am not going to have your
finger in my till a second time." I have
heard that style of talk, have not you?
Did you ever *feel* like it yourself? If you

have, go home and pray to God to get such a feeling out of you, for it is bad stuff to harbour in your soul. You cannot take such hard selfishness to heaven, and it is a great defilement to you on earth. When the Lord Jesus Christ has forgiven you so freely, are you to take your fellow-servant by the throat and say, "Pay me what thou owest?" God forbid that we should continue in such a temper. Be pitiful, easily entreated, ready to forgive. It is a deal better that you should suffer a wrong than do a wrong : much better that you should overlook a fault which you might have noticed, than notice a fault which you ought to have overlooked.

I want to bring forward one more point, and then I have done. If the mysterious providence of God was to be seen in Onesimus getting to Rome, may there not be a providence in your reading this book at this time, or in your being at this hour where you may hear the gospel? People come to the Tabernacle who never meant to come. If anyone had prophesied that they would listen to the gospel they would have poured contempt upon the prophecy, and yet they come. With all manner of twists and turns they have

gone about, but they have been landed
where the truth is proclaimed. Did you
ever miss a train, and so step in to a service
to while away the time? Was the sailing
of your ship delayed when you little expected it, and so were you able to hear a
sermon? I do pray you, then, consider this
question with your own heart—" Does not
God mean to bless me? Has he not given
me an opportunity to yield my heart to
Jesus as Onesimus did?" My dear friend,
if thou believest on the Lord Jesus Christ,
thou shalt have immediate pardon for all
sin, and shalt be saved. The Lord has
brought thee in his infinite wisdom where
thou canst hear his loving invitation,
and I hope that he has also brought
thee where thou wilt accept it, and
so go thy way altogether changed. Some
three years ago I was talking with
an aged minister: he began fumbling
about in his waistcoat pocket, but he was
a long while before he found what he
wanted. At last he brought out a letter
that was well-nigh worn to pieces, and as
he unfolded it, he exclaimed, "God Almighty bless you! God Almighty bless
you!" I said, "Friend, what is it?" He
said, "I had a son. I thought he would

be the stay of my old age, but he disgraced himself, and he went away from
me, and I could not tell where he went,
only he said he was going to America. He
took a ticket to sail for America from the
London Docks, but the ship did not sail
on the day appointed." This aged minister bade me read the letter, and I read
it, and it ran like this :—" Father, I
am here in America. I have found a
situation, and God has prospered me. I
write to ask your forgiveness for the
thousand wrongs that I have done you.
and the grief I have caused you, for,
blessed be God, I have found the Saviour.
I have joined the church of God here, and
hope to spend my life in the Redeemer's
service. It happened thus : I did not sail
for America on the day I expected to start,
and having a leisure hour I went down
to the Tabernacle to see what it was like,
and there God met with me. Mr. Spurgeon
said, 'Perhaps there is a runaway son
here. The Lord call him by his grace.'
And he did call me." " Now," said the
old gentleman, as he folded up the letter
and put it into his pocket, " that son of
mine is dead, and he is in heaven, and I
love you, and I shall do so as long as I

live, because you were the means of bringing him to Christ." Do I speak to a
similar character, or does one of that sort
read these pages? The Lord in mercy
gives you another opportunity of turning
from the error of your ways. I pray you
lift your eye at once to heaven, and say,
" God be merciful to me a sinner," and
he will accept you. Believe in the sinner's
Saviour and he will be *your* Saviour.
Then go home to your father and tell him
what the grace of God has done for you,
and make him wonder at the love which
brought you to Christ.

Thus have we brought before you another
wonder of grace. Our soul longs, yea,
even faints to hear of others in like manner
reclaimed. O poor unsaved souls, by the
love of Jesus we pray you turn unto him
and live. God save you by his Holy
Spirit. Amen.

# THE
# GREATEST WONDER OF ALL

"And I was left."—Ezekiel ix. 8.

SALVATION never shines so brightly to any man's eyes as when it comes to himself. Then is grace illustrious indeed when we can see it working with divine power upon ourselves. To our apprehension, our own case is ever the most desperate, and mercy shown to us is the most extraordinary. We see others perish, and wonder that the same doom has not befallen ourselves. The horror of the ruin which we dreaded, and our intense delight at the certainty of safety in Christ unite with our personal sense of unworthiness to make us cry in amazement, "And I was left."

Ezekiel, in vision, saw the slaughter-

men smiting right and left at the bidding
of divine justice, and as he stood unharmed
among the heaps of the slain, he exclaimed
with surprise, "I was left." It may be,
the day will come when we, too, shall cry
with solemn joy, "And I, too, by sovereign grace, am spared while others perish."
Special grace will cause us to marvel.
Especially will it be so at the last dread
day.

Read the story of the gross idolatry of
the people of Jerusalem, as recorded in the
eighth chapter of Ezekiel's prophecy, and
you will not wonder at the judgment with
which the Lord at length overthrew the
city. Let us set our hearts to consider
how the Lord dealt with the guilty people.
"Six men came from the way of the higher
gate, which lieth toward the north, and
every man with a slaughter weapon in his
hand." The destruction wrought by these
executioners was swift and terrible, and it
was typical of other solemn visitations.
All through history the observing eye
notices lines of justice, red marks upon
the page where the Judge of all the earth
has at last seen it needful to decree a
terrible visitation upon a guilty people.
All these past displays of divine ven-

geance point at a coming judgment even more complete and overwhelming. The past is prophetic of the future. A day is surely coming when the Lord Jesus, who came once to save, will descend a second time to judge. Despised mercy has always been succeeded by deserved wrath, and so must it be in the end of all things. "But who may abide the day of his coming? or who shall stand when he appeareth?" When sinners are smitten, who will be left? He shall lift the balances of justice, and make bare the sword of execution. When his avenging angels shall gather the vintage of the earth, who among us shall exclaim in wondering gratitude, "And I was left"? Such an one will be a wonder of grace indeed; worthy to take rank with those marvels of grace of whom we have spoken in the former discourses of this book. Reader, will you be an instance of sparing grace, and cry, "And I was left"?

We will use the wonderfully descriptive vision of this chapter that we may with holy fear behold *the character of the doom* from which grace delivers us, and then we will dwell upon the exclamation of our text, "I was left," considering it as the joyful utterance of *the persons who are privileged to escape the destruction.*

By the help of the Holy Spirit, let us first solemnly consider THE TERRIBLE DOOM from which the prophet in vision saw himself preserved, regarding it as a figure of the judgment which is yet to come upon all the world.

Observe, first, that it was a *just* punishment inflicted upon those who had been often warned ; a punishment which they wilfully brought upon themselves. God had said that if they set up idols he would destroy them, for he would not endure such an insult to his Godhead. He had often pleaded with them, not with words only, but with severe providences, for their land had been laid desolate, their city had been besieged, and their kings had been carried away captive ; but they were bent on backsliding to the worship of their idol gods. Therefore, when the sword of the Lord was drawn from its scabbard, it was no novel punishment, no freak of vengeance, no unexpected execution. So, in the close of life, and at the end of the world, when judgment comes on men, it will be just and according to the solemn warnings of the word of God.

When I read the terrible things which are written in God's book in reference to future punishment, especially the awful things which Jesus spoke concerning the place where their worm dieth not and their fire is not quenched, I am greatly pressed in spirit.   Some there be who sit in judgment upon the great Judge, and condemn the punishment which he inflicts as too severe.   As for myself, I cannot measure the power of God's anger; but let it burn as it may, I am sure that it will be just.   No needless pang will be inflicted upon a single one of God's creatures : even those who are doomed for ever will endure no more than justice absolutely requires, no more than they themselves would admit to be the due reward of their sins, if their consciences would judge aright. Mark you, this is the very hell of hell that men will know that they are justly suffering.   To endure a tyrant's wrath would be a small thing compared with suffering what one has brought upon himself by wilful wanton choice of wrong. Sin and suffering are indissolubly bound together in the constitution of nature ; it cannot be otherwise, nor ought it to be. It is right that evil should be punished.

Those who were punished in Jerusalem
could not turn upon the executioners
and say, " We do not deserve this doom ;"
but every cruel wound of the Chaldean
sword and every fierce crash of the
Babylonian battle-axe fell on men who
in their consciences knew that they were
only reaping what they themselves had
sown.   Brethren, what wonders of grace
shall we be if from a judgment which we
have so richly deserved we shall be rescued
at the last !

Let us notice very carefully that this
slaughter was *preceded by a separation* which
removed from among the people those who
were distinct in character.   Before the
slaughtermen proceeded to their stern task
a man appeared among them clothed in linen
with a writer's inkhorn by his side, who
marked all those who in their hearts were
grieved at the evil done in the city.   Until
these were marked the destroyers did not
commence their work.   Whenever the
Lord lays bare his arm for war he first
gathers his saints into a place of safety.
He did not destroy the world by the flood
till Noah and his family were safe in the
ark.   He would not suffer a single fire-
drop to fall on Sodom till Lot had

escaped to Zoar. He carefully preserves his own; nor flood nor flame, nor pestilence nor famine shall do them ill. We read in the Revelation that the angel said, "Hurt not the earth, neither the sea, nor the trees, till we have sealed the servants of our God in their foreheads." Vengeance must sheathe her sword, till love has housed its darlings. When Christ cometh to destroy the earth, he will first catch away his people. Ere the elements shall melt with fervent heat, and the pillars of the universe shall rock and reel beneath the weight of wrathful deity, he will have caught up his elect into the air so that they shall be ever with the Lord. When he cometh he shall divide the nations as a shepherd divideth his sheep from the goats; no sheep of his shall be destroyed: he shall without fail take the tares from among the wheat, but not one single ear of wheat shall be in danger. O that we may be among the selected ones and prove his power to keep us in the day of wrath. May each one of us say amid the wreck of matter and the crash of worlds, "And I was left." Dear friend, are you marked in the forehead, think you? If at this moment my voice were drowned by the trumpet of resurrection, would you be amongst those who awake to safety and glory? Would you be able to say, "The multitude perished around me, but I was left"? It will be so if you hate the sins by which you are surrounded, and if you have received the mark of the blood of Jesus upon your souls; if not, you will not escape, for there is no other door of salvation but his saving name. God grant us grace to belong to that chosen number who wear the covenant seal, the mark of him who counteth up the people.

Next, this judgment was placed *in the Mediator's hands.* I want you to notice this. Observe that, according to the chapter, there was no slaughter done except where the man with the writer's inkhorn led the way. So again we read in the tenth chapter, that " One cherub stretched forth his hand from between the cherubims unto the fire that was between the cherubims, and took thereof and put it into the hands of him that was clothed with linen ; who took it, and went out," and cast it over the city. See you this. God's glory of old shone forth between the cherubim, that is to say, over the place of

propitiation and atonement, and as long
as that glow of light remained no judgment fell on Jerusalem, for God in Christ
condemns not.    But by-and-by " The
glory of the God of Israel was gone up
from the cherub, whereupon he was, to the
threshold of the house," and then judgment was near to come.    When God no
longer deals with men in Christ his wrath
burns like fire, and he commissions the
ambassador of mercy to be the messenger of
wrath.    The very man who marked with his
pen the saved ones threw burning coals
upon the city and led the way for the destruction of the sinful.    What does this
teach but this—" The Father judgeth no
man, but hath committed all judgment
unto the Son "?    I know of no truth more
dreadful to meditate upon.    Think of it,
ye careless ones: the very Christ who died
on Calvary is he by whom you will be
sentenced.    God will judge the world by
this man Christ Jesus : he it is that will
come in the clouds of heaven, and before
him shall be gathered all nations ; and
when those who have despised him shall
look upon his face they will be terrified
beyond conception.    Not the lightnings,
not the thunders, not the dreadful sound

of the last tremendous trump shall so
alarm them as that face of injured love.
Then will they cry to the mountains and
hills to hide them from the face of him
that sitteth upon the throne. Why, it is
the face of him that wept for sinners, the
face which scoffers stained with bloody
drops extracted by the thorny crown, the
face of the incarnate God who, in infinite mercy, came to save mankind! But
because they have despised him, because
they would not be saved, because they
preferred their own lusts to infinite love,
and would persist in rejecting God's best
proof of kindness, therefore will they say,
" Hide us from the face," for the sight
of that face shall be to them more ac-
cusing, and more condemning, than all
else besides. How dreadful is this truth!
The more you consider it, the more will it
fill your soul with terror! Would to God
it might drive you to fly to Jesus, for
then you will behold him with joy in that
day.

This destruction, we are told, *began at
the sanctuary*. Suppose the Lord were to
visit London in his anger, where would
he begin to smite? "Oh," somebody
says," of course the destroying angel would

**go** down to the low music halls and dancing rooms, or he would sweep out the back slums and the drink palaces, the jails and places where women of ill life do congregate." Turn to the Scripture which surrounds our text. The Lord says, "Begin at my sanctuary." Begin at the churches, begin at the chapels, begin at the church members, begin at the ministers, begin at the bishops, begin at those who are teachers of the gospel. Begin at the chief and front of the religious world, begin at the high professors who are looked up to as examples. What does Peter say? "The time is come that judgment must begin at the house of God: and if it first begin at us, what shall the end be of them that obey not the gospel of God? And if the righteous scarcely be saved, where shall the ungodly and the sinner appear?"

The first thing the slaughtermen did was to slay the ancient men which were before the temple, even the seventy elders of the people, for they were secret idolaters. You may be sure that the sword which did not spare the chief men and fathers made but short work with the baser sort. Elders of our churches, ministers of Christ, judgment will begin with us; we must not expect to find more lenient treatment than others at the last great assize; nay, rather, if there shall be a specially careful testing of sincerity it will be for us who have taken upon ourselves to lead others to the Saviour. For this cause let us see well to it that we be not deceived or deceivers, for we shall surely be detected in that day. To play the hypocrite is to play the fool. Will a man deceive his Maker, or delude the Most High? It cannot be. You church members, all of you, should look well to it, for judgment will begin with you. God's fire is in Zion and his furnace in Jerusalem. In the olden time the people fled to churches and holy places for sanctuary; but how vain will this be when the Lord's avengers shall come forth, since there the havoc will begin! How fiercely shall the sword sweep through the hosts of carnal professors, the men who called themselves servants of God, while they were slaves of the devil; who drank of the cup of the Lord but were drunken with the wine of their own lusts: who could lie and cheat and commit fornication, and yet dared to approach the sacred table of the Lord? What cutting and hewing will there be among the base-born professors of our churches! It were better for such men that they had never been born, or, being born, that their lot had fallen amid heathen ignorance, so that they might have been unable to add sin to sin by lying unto the living God. "Begin at my sanctuary." The word is terrible to all those who have a name to live and are dead. God grant that in such testing times when many fail we may survive every ordeal and through grace exclaim in the end, "And I was left."

After the executioners had begun at the sanctuary it is to be observed that they *did not spare any except those upon whom was the mark.* Old and young, men and women, priests and people, all were slain who had not the sacred sign; and so in the last tremendous day all sinners who have not fled to Christ will perish. Our dear babes that died in infancy we believe to be all washed in the blood of Jesus and all saved; but for the rest of mankind who have lived to years of responsibility there will be only one of two things—they must either be saved because they had faith in Christ, or else the full weight of divine wrath must fall upon them. Either the mark of Christ's pen or of Christ's sword must be upon every one. There will be no sparing of one man because he was rich, nor of another because he was learned, nor of a third because he was eloquent, nor of a fourth because he was held in high esteem. Those who are marked with the blood of Christ are safe! Without that mark all are lost! This is the one separating sign—do you wear it? Or will you die in your sins? Bow down at once before the feet of Jesus and beseech him to mark you as his own, that so you may be one of those who will joyfully cry, "And I was left."

Now, secondly, I have to call your very particular attention to THE PERSONS WHO ESCAPED, who could each say, "And I was left." We are told that those were marked for mercy who did "sigh and cry for the abominations that were done in the midst thereof." Now we must be very particular about this. It is no word of mine, remember: it is God's word, and therefore I beg you to hear and weigh it for yourselves. We do not read that the devouring sword passed by those quiet people who never did anybody any harm: no mention is made of such an exemption.

Neither does the record say that the Lord saved those professors who were judicious, and maintained a fair name and repute until death. No; the only people that were saved were those who were exercised in heart, and that heart-work was of a painful kind : they sighed and cried because of abounding sin. They saw it, protested against it, avoided it, and last of all wept over it continually. Where testimony failed it remained for them to mourn ; retiring from public labours they sat them down and sighed their hearts away because of the evils which they could not cure ; and when they felt that sighing alone would do no good they took to crying in prayer to God that he would come and put an end to the dreadful ills which brooded over the land. I would not say a hard thing, but I wonder, if I were able to read the secret lives of professors of religion whether I should find that they all sigh and cry over the sins of others ? Are the tenth of them thus engaged ? I am afraid that it does not cause some people much anxiety when they see sin rampant around them. They say that they are sorry, but it never frets them much, or causes them as much trouble as would come of a lost sixpence or a cut finger. Did you ever feel as if your heart would break over an ungodly son? I do not believe that you are a Christian man if you have such a son and have not felt an agony on his behalf. Did you ever feel as if you could lay down your life to save that daughter of yours? I cannot believe that you are a Christian woman if you have not sometimes come to that. When you have gone through the street and heard an oath, has not your blood chilled in you? has not horror taken hold upon you because of the wicked? There cannot be much grace in you if that has not been the case. If you can go up and down in the world fully at ease because you are prospering in business, and things go smoothly with you, if you forget the woe of this city's sin and poverty, and the yet greater woe which cometh upon it, how dwelleth the love of God in you? The saving mark is only set on those who sigh and cry, and if you are heartless and indifferent there is no such mark on you. "Are we to be always miserable?" asks one. Far from it. There are many other things to make us rejoice, but if the sad state of our fellow men does not cause us to sigh and cry, then we have not the grace of God in us. "Well," says one, "but every man must look to himself." That is the language of Cain—"Am I my brother's keeper?" That kind of talk is in keeping with the spirit of the wicked one and his seed, but the heir of heaven abhors such language. The genuine Christian loves his race, and therefore he longs to see it made holy and happy. He cannot bear to see men sinning, and so dishonouring God and ruining themselves. If we really love the Lord we shall sometimes lie awake at night sighing to think how his name is blasphemed, and how little progress his gospel makes. We shall groan to think that men should despise the glorious God who made them, and who daily loads them with benefits. It sometimes lies upon my heart like a huge mountain which crushes my spirit to think that Jesus should be rejected, and that in this land of Bibles, where Latimer lit a candle which shall never be put out, the old madness is returning, and many are again bowing before the images of jealousy which the priests have set up. Yes, we have priests among us again. You can see them in their long and ugly garments in every street. And women have begun to confess to them! Shame! Shame! I marvel that the crimson blush does not mantle the cheek of every one who dares to ask or answer the questions appointed for the confessional, and yet the questions are asked, and modesty is outraged, and the multitudes tamely look on. My countrymen are going back to Rome. Their fathers' noble blood was shed for God, and none was left for the veins of their sons. In vain the conflicts of the years gone by! In vain a Cromwell's mighty arm and the purging of the land! In vain the Puritans driven from their pulpits and witnessing in poverty and persecution! England must needs go back again to wear the fetters forged by papal Rome. My God, prevent it! Prevent it if it cost the lives of thousands of us, for we would be glad to die to save our country from so dire a curse. If you never sigh and cry because of the spread of Ritualism, I do not understand you. What stuff are you made of? "Oh, but my business goes on exceedingly well." Yes, and so does mine when souls are saved, but when they are led away into error my business cannot prosper, but I have loss upon loss. I am happy enough when I think Christ's kingdom comes; but nothing beneath the sky can give me solid satisfaction if my Lord's work is at a standstill. I would to God we were all so taken up with the glory of God that the wickedness of mankind would grieve us to the heart.

But it was not their mourning which saved those who escaped—it was the mark which they all received which preserved them from destruction. We must all bear the mark of Jesus Christ. What is that? It is the mark of faith in the atoning blood. That sets apart the chosen of the Lord, and that alone. If you have that mark—and you have it not unless you sigh and cry over the sins of others—then in that last day no sword of justice can come near you. Did you read that word, "But come not nigh any man upon whom is the mark." Come not even near the marked ones lest they be afraid. The grace-marked man is safe even from the near approach of ill. Christ bled for him, and therefore he cannot, must not, die. Let him alone, ye bearers of the destroying weapons. Just as the angel of death, when he flew through the land of Egypt, was forbidden to touch a house where the blood of the lamb was on the lintel and the two side posts, so is it sure that avenging justice cannot touch the man who is in Christ Jesus. Who is he that condemneth since Christ has died? Have you, then, the blood mark? Yes or no. Do not refuse to question yourself upon this point. Do not take it for granted, lest you be deceived. Believe me, your all hangs upon it. If you are not registered by the man clothed in linen you will not be able to say, "And I was left."

This brings me to this last point which I desire to speak of. *What were the prophet's emotions when he said, "And I was left"?* He saw men falling right and left, and *he* himself stood like a lone rock amidst a sea of blood; and he cried in wonder, "And I was left."

Let us hear what he further says—"I fell on my face." He lay prostrate with *humility*. Have you a hope that you are saved? Fall on your face, then! See the hell from which you are delivered, and bow before the Lord. Why are you to be saved more than anyone else? Certainly not because of any merit in you. It is

due to the sovereign grace of God alone.
Fall on your face and own your indebtedness.

" Why was I made to hear thy voice,
    And enter while there's room,
    When thousands make a wretched choice,
    And rather starve than come?"

" And I was left."

If a man has been a drunkard, and has
at length been led to flee to Christ, when
he says, " And I was left," he will feel the
hot tears rising to his eyes, for many other
drinkers have died in delirium.   One who
has been a public sinner, when she is saved
will not be able to think of it without astonishment.   Indeed, each saved man is a
marvel to himself.   Nobody here wonders
more at divine grace in his salvation than
I do myself.   Why was I chosen, and
called, and saved ?   I cannot make it out,
and I never shall ; but I will always praise,
and bless, and magnify my **Lord** for cast-
ing an eye of love upon me.   Will you not
do the same, beloved, if you feel that you
by grace are left ?   Will you not fall on
your face and bless the mercy which makes
you to differ ?

What did the prophet do next ?   Finding

that he was left he began to pray for others. "Ah, Lord," said he, "wilt thou destroy all the residue of Israel?" Intercession is an instinct of the renewed heart. When the believer finds that he is safe he must pray for his fellow-men. Though the prophet's prayer was too late, yet, blessed be God, ours will not be. We shall be heard. Pray, then, for perishing men. Ask God, who has spared you, to spare those who are like you. Somebody has said, there will be three great wonders in heaven, first, to see so many there whom we never expected to meet in glory; secondly, to miss so many of whom we felt sure that they must be safe; and thirdly, the greatest wonder of all will be to find ourselves there. I am sure that every one who has a hope of being in glory feels it to be a marvel; and he resolves, "If I am saved, I will sing the loudest of them all, for I shall owe most to the abounding mercy of God."

Let me ask a few questions, and I have done. The first—and let each man ask it of himself—shall I be left when the ungodly are slain? Answer it now to yourselves. Men, women, children, will you be spared in that last great day? Are you in Christ? Have you a good hope in him? Do not lie unto yourselves. You will be weighed in the balances; will you be found wanting or not? "Shall I be left?" Let that question burn into your souls.

Next, will my relatives be saved? My wife, my husband, my children, my brother, my sister, my father, my mother—will these all be saved? Happy are we who can say, "Yes, we believe they will," as some of us can joyfully hope. But if you have to say, "No, I fear that my boy is unconverted, or that my father is unsaved;" then do not rest till you have wrestled with God for their salvation. Good woman, if you are obliged to say, "I fear my husband is unconverted," join me in prayer. Bow your heads at once and cry unto your God, "Lord, save our children! Lord, save our parents! Lord, save our husbands and wives, our brothers and sisters; and let the whole of our families meet in heaven, unbroken circles, for thy name's sake!"

May God hear that prayer if it has come from the lips of sincerity! I could not endure the thought of missing one of my boys in heaven : I hope I shall see them both there, and therefore I am in deep sympathy with any of you who have not seen your households brought to Christ. O for grace to pray earnestly and labour zealously for the salvation of your whole households.

The next earnest enquiry is, if you and your relatives are saved, how about your neighbours, your fellow-workmen, your companions in business ? "Oh," say you, "many of them are scoffers. A good many of them are still in the gall of bitterness." A sorrowful fact, but have you spoken to them ? It is wonderful what a kind word will do ? Have you tried it ? Did you ever try to speak to that person who meets you every morning as you go to work ? Suppose he should be lost ! Oh, it will be a bitter feeling for you to think that he went down to the pit without your making an effort to bring him to God. Do not let it be so. "But we must not be too pushing," says one. I do not know about that. If you saw poor people in a burning house nobody would blame you for being officious if you helped to save them. When a man is sinking in the river, if you jump in and pull him out nobody will say, "You were rude and intrusive, for you were never introduced to him!" This world has been lost, and it must be saved ; and we must not mind manners in saving it. We must get a grip of sinking sinners somehow, even if it be by the hair of their heads, ere they sink, for if they sink they are lost for ever. They will forgive us very soon for any roughness that we use ; but we shall not forgive ourselves if, for want of a little energy, we permit them to die without a knowledge of the truth.

Oh, beloved friends, if you are left while others perish, I beseech you, by the mercies of God, by the bowels of compassion which are in Christ Jesus, by the bleeding wounds of the dying Son of God, do love your fellow men, and sigh and cry about them if you cannot bring them to Christ. If you cannot save them you can weep over them. If you cannot give them a drop of cold water in hell, you can give them your heart's tears while yet they are in this body.

But are you in very deed reconciled to God yourselves ? Reader, are you cured of the awful disease of sin ? Are you marked with the blood-red sign of trust in the atoning blood? Do you believe in the Lord Jesus Christ? If not, the Lord have mercy upon you! May you have sense enough to have mercy upon yourself. May the Spirit of God instruct you to that end. Amen.